CREATIVE
COINCIDENCES

CREATIVE COINCIDENCES

The Next Phase of Human Evolution

Influence the Coincidences in Your Life

José Silva
and Ed Bernd Jr.

Introduction by José Silva Jr.

ebook and Audio book are available from G&D Media.

For more genuine Jose Silva books and products please visit
SilvaMethodUltraMind.com

Edited by David Aretha
Interior design by Meghan Day Healey of Story Horse, LLC

Library of Congress Cataloging-in-Publication Data is available upon request

ISBN: 978-1-965725-02-3 (Paperback)
ISBN: 978-1-965725-03-0 (Hardcover)
ISBN: 978-1-965725-04-7 (Hardcover Large Print Edition)

10 9 8 7 6 5 4 3 2 1

Contents

PART THREE
Explanations

Science Discovers Where Good Luck Comes From

by José Silva Jr.

Have you ever wondered why some people seem to be so much luckier than everybody else?

My father was one of those lucky people. When he saw other people working just as hard as he was but not getting the same results, he decided to see if he could figure out why.

He said that the coincidences throughout his life that led to the development of the Silva Method and his UltraMind ESP Systems were no accident. "We were guided every step of the way," he said, "and that's putting it lightly."

He invested twenty-two years and half a million dollars of his own money in scientific research to learn how the brain and mind work.

Then he began teaching a course named Silva Mind Control that was based on his research findings.

And he kept studying, seeking the final piece of the puzzle. It was revealed to him less than two years before his passing. He called it the MentalVideo Technique.

How to Read This Book

To get started, read the first three chapters, and you will know how to use the MentalVideo tonight to obtain the guidance and help you need from higher intelligence.

Chapter 1: How to prepare yourself for success

Chapter 2: What you must do to succeed

Chapter 3: The MentalVideo formula you can use tonight

Then for more ideas and guidance, examples, case studies, and answers to your questions, go to any chapter you are interested in. After the first three chapters, you can skip around if you wish. Just read the first three chapters first.

Examples and Case Studies

In the second section of the book you will meet people from all walks of life and see how they attracted positive life-changing coincidences:

- An unemployed thirty-five-year-old was guided to his ideal job, and how it was a springboard to finding his life purpose.
- Coincidences guided desperate people to decent housing during challenging times.
- A senior citizen's prayers were answered, fulfilling his life-long dream of winning the World Series as manager of a major league baseball team.

- A woman encountered her old doctor unexpectedly in a parking lot and got exactly the medical help she needed as a result.
- An overworked father was guided to a winning lottery ticket.
- A Silva UltraMind student in Bulgaria resolved a legal dispute with the help of the MentalVideo Technique.
- How jet lag, a live news report on television in the middle of the night, and desire to see peace in the world may have influenced world events in a positive way.
- Higher intelligence helps detectives solve a murder.

The Second Phase of Human Evolution on the Planet

Imagine a world filled with:

Abundance: Everybody knows how to get whatever they need without taking from others or hurting anybody.

Wisdom: We quickly resolve differences through shared knowledge and by seeking guidance from higher intelligence.

Peace: War is no longer possible because we can detect anyone's ill intent and stop it before it begins.

It would truly be a paradise on earth.

The MentalVideo Technique is the culmination of my father's fifty-five years of scientific research and experience in this field. It is the technique that is leading humanity into what he called the "second phase of human evolution on the planet."

The first phase was to develop our physical abilities and tame the physical world.

We have gone about as far as we can go with that. The old ways of "survival of the fittest" are no longer working. Our social and political institutions are breaking down and failing us.

What we need is a spiritual awakening.

And that means: We must find out what higher intelligence wants us to do, and how to go about doing it.

"The reason we were given psychic ability," he told us, "is to use it to find out what we were sent here to do and how to do it successfully."

Fulfill Your Mission in Life

Have you ever felt like there was something more you should be doing with your life? Maybe you have a hidden talent just ready to burst into success. Or a special mission, a soul purpose, you are ready to achieve?

Imagine having a guide who knows what lies ahead for you, who can help you achieve the success you know you deserve.

That's what the Silva UltraMind ESP Systems are all about: To help you achieve the success you know that you are capable of achieving, and make the rest of your life the best of your life.

My Father's Prescription for a Successful Life:
- Maintain a perfectly healthy body and mind
- Solve problems and do worthwhile things
- Leave behind a better world for those who follow

"The world was not created for just one person," he told us. We must do what we can to correct problems—our own problems, and any other problems we become aware of.

When you are solving problems, and you use the MentalVideo Technique, you will receive guidance and help from higher intelligence.

Start Reaping Benefits Right Now

There's no prerequisite, no prior experience required to use the MentalVideo. You just need a:

- willingness to follow simple instructions
- desire to solve problems and improve living conditions for yourself and others

Now here to guide you is Ed Bernd Jr., coauthor of my father's last four books.

As my father would say: "May the rest of your life be the *best* of your life."

PART ONE

The
Silva MentalVideo

CHAPTER 1

Help from a Higher Power

A spontaneous event with detrimental end results is an accident.

A series of accidents tells us that we're doing something wrong. Either we are not getting intuitive guidance or we are being advised that we are going in the wrong direction.

A spontaneous event with beneficial end results is a coincidence. This could be good luck, or it could be divine guidance.

How can we be sure that it is divine guidance?

A series of coincidences on the same subject is surely divine intervention. Nobody working on their own is lucky every time.

Divine intervention is what is known as God helping without showing His hand.

—JOSÉ SILVA

What Would You Ask For?

If you had a reliable way to communicate with a higher power—a scientific way to pray—what would you ask of "higher intelligence"?

- Do you want a better job?
- A raise? More money?
- Something more meaningful, interesting, and satisfying to do?
- How about your own business?
- More customers?
- Bigger sales?
- Better employees?
- Better working conditions?
- More free time?

Bad decisions lead to disappointment, unhappiness, suffering, failure.

Good decisions bring success, happiness, respect, love.

Success Is Waiting for You

How would it change your life if you had a tutor to help you make the right decisions, and guide you toward your mission in life?

You already have a tutor with the ability to lead you to the success you know, deep within, that you are capable of. Now you need a reliable way to communicate with your tutor and ask for the right thing at the right time and in the right manner.

In the next chapter we will explain what kind of requests higher intelligence will help you with, and how and when to submit your requests.

Do Your Part

You need to do your part, of course. You must first try to solve the problem yourself. We have books and courses with plenty of techniques.

José Silva's Choose Success Master Course book has techniques for simple things like: stop smoking, fall asleep without drugs and wake up without clocks, relieve nervousness, stop excessive drinking, memorize long lists, and improve creativity.

His newest course, the Silva UltraMind ESP System, helps you learn the more sophisticated things like develop ESP and use it to get information, make better decisions, and create more solutions. There is information in the Appendix about additional Silva books and courses.

In order to qualify for help from higher intelligence you need to ask for the right things.

You need to ask at the right time, and in the right manner.

Now let's turn the floor over to José Silva to explain what kind of help we can qualify for.

CHAPTER 2

How to Get Help from Higher Intelligence

by José Silva

If you want help from higher intelligence, your goals should be not just benefits for you and yours. Animals do that.

We want to also help other human beings.

You see, animals take care of themselves and their offspring, but animals don't help other animals of the same species.

That is what many humans are doing right now: They don't care about anybody else. But we *should* care about other human beings also. We cannot survive by ourselves.

We need shops to manufacture shoes for us because we don't manufacture shoes ourselves; clothing because we don't manufacture clothing. I pay somebody to change the oil in my auto.

We need each other. It is not just about me, and forget everybody else. All our plans should be considered as "we," or "us"; meaning:

Humanity is not just me and my immediate family. Animals do that automatically; they don't even have to have intelligence to supply their needs and the needs of their immediate family.

We want to go beyond that. Not just what animals are capable of doing; we want to be able to do what humans are capable of doing with the intelligence that we have, way beyond what animals are capable of doing.

The Highest Level of Intelligence

We are the highest level of intelligence on the planet.

Animals don't have a human mind.

The analytical factor is what makes the difference between a human being and an animal.

We human beings have the analytical factor in our favor.

The human mind, with the deductive faculty, the analytical factor, is what does it all.

How to Qualify for Help from Higher Intelligence

Now that you understand our mission you are on the right track. Now you can ask for help and get it.

It is about what your intentions are. You are walking down the street tomorrow and see a board with a nail sticking out. Ninety-nine percent of the people walk by, just kick it aside, saying, "Somebody's going to get hurt with that. Let them take care of it—what the heck do I care about it."

Yes, you should care. You should pick it up, get the nail out of the way before somebody gets hurt. This is how we are supposed to be functioning on this planet, and we're not. We don't care for one another.

"Love one another" means "help one another." You help me and I'll help you. We all help each other would be great.

CHAPTER 3

The MentalVideo Technique

If you have a problem you are stuck with, and if the solution you need complies with the Laws of Programming, then you can use the MentalVideo tonight to request help from higher intelligence.

This formula-type technique guides you to present your request at the right time and in the right way.

Be sure to follow these step-by-step instructions exactly as written while you are first learning. Once you have had some successes with it, then you can shorten the procedure.

If you know how to enter the alpha brainwave level you can get even better results. If you don't know how, we explain in Chapter 16. You can read it now or later, your choice.

The MentalVideo is a scientific way to pray: It uses two requirements of "scientific method":

- Replication (repeatability)
- Objective (physical) feedback

The guidance you receive will be in a physical form, something you can "see" with your eyes. If you get an idea and think it might be your "indication," then you can act on it and observe the results in the physical world.

If you want to confirm the guidance you receive, then you can create a new MentalVideo and see if the results are consistent.

Requirements to Keep in Mind:

There are two requirements to keep in mind:

It is not our place to put God to work, so it is important that you do your part and try to solve the problem yourself. However, if you have developed a plan and would like for higher intelligence to review it for you, that is okay. It is better to prevent problems and concentrate on solutions.

You must comply with the Laws of Programming. Here they are:

Laws of Programming

The following laws are to be considered when programming:

- You should do to others only what you like others to do to you.
- The solution must help to make this planet a better place to live.
- It must be the best for everybody concerned.
- It must help at least two or more persons.
- It must be within the possibility area.

How to Qualify for Help When You Need It

When you need help, or when you want to make sure that what you are doing is what God wants you to do, you can use the MentalVideo Technique.

José Silva said, "We are like fingers on the hand of God. We are here to carry out the work that higher intelligence wants done."

That's why we don't do what some "self-improvement" programs do:

They just talk about taking care of yourself. José Silva never said that. You might need to solve some of your own problems so that you can then be strong enough and healthy enough to help others.

Your reason for wanting to get healthy and stay healthy is so you can be a better problem solver, improve living conditions on the planet, and help to make the planet a better world to live in for all of us, for your loved ones, and for other people as well.

We're all in this together, and sometimes we need to forgo personal benefit for the greater good.

"The world was not made for just one person," Mr. Silva said, "but every person was made for the world."

We see many examples of that:

Something happens somewhere, the supply chain is upset, people panic that they aren't going to be able to get enough toilet paper because the supply chain was disrupted, a factory had a problem.

There are components in your smartphone from many different countries, that travel through many different countries, getting to wherever they're assembled, and the assembled products get to the countries where they're sold.

The MentalVideo Formula:

Whenever you need to solve a problem, make a decision, or obtain guidance with the MentalVideo Technique, proceed in the following manner:

At beta, with your eyes open, mentally create, with visualization, a MentalVideo of a problem, or the existing situation. Include everything that belongs to the animate matter kingdom. Animate matter means everything that contains life.

After you have completed the MentalVideo of the problem, use visualization to review it at beta, with your eyes closed.

Later, when you are in bed and ready to go to sleep, go to your center with the 3-to-1 method. Once you are at your center, review the MentalVideo that you created of the problem, or the existing situation, when you were at the beta level.

After you have reviewed the problem, mentally convert the problem into a project. Then create, with imagination, a Mental-Video of the solution.

The MentalVideo of the solution should contain a step-by-step procedure of how you desire the project to be resolved.

After both of the MentalVideos have been completed, go to sleep with the intention of delivering the MentalVideos to your tutor while you sleep. Take for granted that the delivery will be made.

During the next three days, look for indications that point to the solution. Every time you think of the project, think of the solution that you created in the MentalVideo, in a past tense sense.

A Review of How the Formula Works

The first step in the MentalVideo formula is to create this problem video at the beta level, with your eyes open.

Then review it at the beta level with eyes closed. Do that before you're ready to go to bed.

Then when you're ready to go to sleep, close your eyes, go to the alpha brainwave level as you learn in Chapter 16, and recall the video you created of the problem. If you don't know how to go to alpha, just close your eyes and relax.

Then create a solution video: Picture yourself healthy, working, doing your job. Imagine yourself taking care of your children, taking them to school, or whatever it is that you do.

Exaggerate Your Solution Video

We exaggerate our fear, don't we? You can program yourself mentally that whenever you think of something bad happening, you will immediately cancel that thought by saying "Cancel-cancel" and replace it with a positive thought—of good health, prosperity, or solutions that you are working on.

Before you go to sleep, imagine delivering those two videos—the problem video and the solution video—to higher intelligence, to your assistant, to your "tutor," we call it, on the other side.

Your tutor would be what a religious person would call an angel, a helper of God.

How to Make Your MentalVideos

You can imagine using your smartphone to make a video of the problem.

Maybe you have a friend who is sick. Make a short Mental-Video of the problem: Show how you have been trying to help them, and they're not improving or improving so slowly.

Or it may be for yourself. Turn your smartphone around, make a selfie, create a short problem video showing that you need to do your job, support your family, help others who need help.

Picture that problem, create a video. Doesn't have to be a long video. Just say, "Oh, I got the symptoms, the sniffles, the aches and pain. This is what I've got."

Just a quick video. What does that take? Five seconds, ten seconds, and you have a video of the problem.

Some Suggestions to Help You

The formula says, "During the next three days look for indications that point to the solution."

Allow three days to get your results. It may come right away, in the morning when you wake up, or it may come later in the day or the next day or the third day.

Allow yourself three days to get results.

You don't want to go back and make the same request every day, day after day. Give it time to work because it may take time to arrange things in the physical dimension.

You have solved the problem mentally. Mr. Silva told us to "program in the future in a past tense sense." Pray believing you have already received. Mentally, it's a done deal—you have already received the results (in the subjective dimension), and you are just waiting for them to be delivered in the objective dimension.

Physically, we're waiting for results. They'll come, but we still have time and space in the physical dimension. During the next three days, look for indications of how to proceed.

You may see something on the news, hear something on the radio, or a friend may say something to you. Maybe you have an idea and you go on Google and look it up and see the answer you need.

"Oh wow, if I drink prune juice, I bet this will loosen up everything inside. I bet it will solve this problem I've got. That will take the stress off my body so that it can deal with the underlying problem that I haven't been doing so well with. Everything will be fine." It might be just that simple. It might be something you and even your doctor wouldn't have thought about, but it may come to you that way.

That's how the MentalVideo can help us.

How Can We Be Sure It Is Divine Guidance?

José Silva said: "A series of coincidences on the same subject is surely divine intervention. Nobody working on their own is lucky every time. Divine intervention is what is known as God helping without showing His hand."

Where Does the Guidance Come From?

The short answer is that the guidance comes from a higher power that governs the whole universe. This is what some people call God, or Allah, or Jehovah, Yahweh, The Almighty, and many other names.

If you want to know more about José Silva's concept of higher intelligence, also why we do this technique at night, skip forward to Chapter 14 for his explanation.

If you are eager to get started and see some examples, case studies, and tips for improving your results, you can go directly to any of the following chapters.

To Summarize

The main things to keep in mind are:

- Ask for things that will benefit more than just yourself.
- Ask as you are ready to go to sleep.
- Think visually and "show" the problem and your desired solution.

CHAPTER 4

Who Is Your Tutor?

We each have a tutor on the other side who will guide us if we ask
for help:

- at the right time
- the right place
- for the right things
- in the correct manner
- with the correct attitude

The MentalVideo Technique guides you in all of those areas,
and once you learn and have some successes and gain confidence
in the technique and your ability to use it, you can expand your
ability to communicate with your tutor at any time of day or
night.

José Silva was a lifelong Catholic, so he thought in terms of
angels, archangels, and so forth—a hierarchy of intelligences,
much like the hierarchies we see in business, the military, government, and elsewhere.

He said it doesn't make sense that someone intelligent enough to create all of that would have created it in such a way that one God would have to watch everybody every minute of every day.

It makes more sense that God would have established a hierarchy, much as we see here on planet Earth.

Look at our structures in business: You have the president of a company, and you have a whole lot of vice presidents who are responsible for certain activities within the company, for specific territories around the country, around the planet, and each vice president has people who report to him or to her, and each of those people have people reporting to them.

When you go into a store, you buy from a sales clerk, who answers to a department manager, who answers to a sales manager, who answers to a regional vice president, who answers to the president, or whatever the structure may be, depending on the size of the company.

We see the same thing in government: When you need some help, you don't go all the way to the mayor of your city, or to the governor of your state, or to the president of your country. You go to the person who can help you.

If you need help with a parking situation on your street, you simply call the police department. You probably talk to a dispatcher, who will then refer you to someone in the traffic department, who will then go to someone higher up, if necessary, to get the necessary action to take care of things.

As long as they take care of the job the mayor never finds out about it. If they don't take care of the job, then it gets passed up the hierarchy, and you go before the city council and you present it to them. You say, "Hey, I need help with this." You go to whatever level you need to go to get the job done.

Mr. Silva felt it is the very same way here. He felt that each of us has a personal representative. Some people think of it as an angel, perhaps, a guardian angel watching over us.

In order to respect everyone's religion, he used a scientific term and referred to it as a tutor, which is a teacher. We turn the MentalVideo over to our tutor.

Now what may happen is that your tutor and my tutor might get together and bring us together, if that's the best way to solve a problem.

UltraMind ESP Systems Definition of Delta:

Here is José Silva's explanation of the purpose of the delta brainwave frequency, the brain frequency associated with the deepest level of sleep, and how he discovered this purpose:

At a specific time after conception, a spiritual human entity enters the fetus, and the brain of the fetus then starts functioning electronically and emitting human-type brain frequencies. This provides proof that a spiritual human entity has arrived. It is said that it came from the spiritual dimension (the other side) where the hierarchy of God resides.

When the brain of a fetus starts functioning electronically it starts producing a slow pulsing frequency that scientists call delta.

The delta pulsing frequency is the slowest that the brain produces and it is the first pulsing frequency that can be detected in the fetus by the electroencephalograph.

Delta is also the last frequency detected at the point of death.

Delta only occupies half an octave in the normal brain frequency spectrum.

Why is this?

It indicates that delta straddles two dimensions, and serves as the door between the spiritual (the other side) and the physical (this side).

Every time we sleep and enter delta, our mind subjectively crosses into the spiritual (other side) where your Tutor and the hierarchy of God reside. It is at this time that MentalVideos can be delivered to your personal Tutor.

SCALE OF BRAIN EVOLUTION

©Copyright 1969-2001 by Jose Silva & Silva UltraMind Systems, LLC, Laredo, Texas U.S.A.

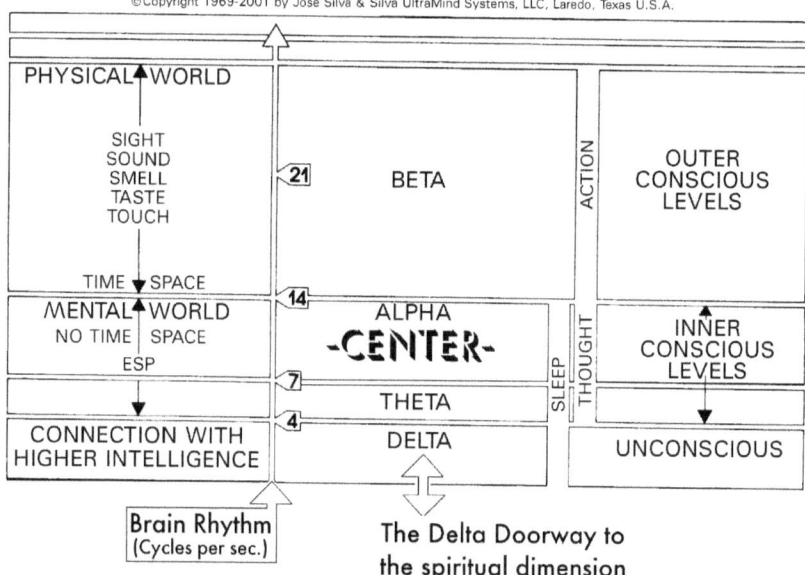

Using Delta During the Day

Mr. Silva confirmed that we can also dip into delta during the day, and receive guidance and help from higher intelligence once we have developed the use of delta by using the MentalVideo Technique at night.

Every time you create a MentalVideo and deliver it to your Tutor while you sleep, you are becoming more and more familiar with how to do it. It is like you are wearing a path back and forth every time you seek guidance and help and get an answer from the other side, and each time it becomes easier.

How does this help you during the day? Let me explain:

When we say your brain functions at certain brain frequencies, what we actually mean is that it is focused on a certain frequency, and using a certain part of the brain. But the rest of your brain is still functioning, even if you are not consciously aware of it.

Because of this, your mind can quickly dip into any frequency at any time, if you have done it before.

So even if you are functioning predominantly in beta and engaged in physical activity, your brain can:

- dip into alpha for a "flash of insight"
- dip into delta to let your Tutor know you need some help

With the MentalVideo, you now have a way to keep your tutor informed.

Now you know why we instruct you to use the MentalVideo at night, as you are going to sleep, while you are learning, and how doing this will make it easy to learn to use it "on the fly" when you need to.

PART TWO

Examples and Case Studies

CHAPTER 5

How to Find a Job and a Whole Lot More

"If you do the right job then money will come to you.
Because people who need you will request, will ask for you, will
attract you, and will be willing to pay you for your services."

—JOSÉ SILVA

A lady named Carla, who was studying the Free Introductory Lessons available at our Silva7.com website, asked a very good question:

"Can you please clarify for me the best way to ask higher intelligence what I should be doing for work right now?

"I have been feeling stifled and stuck due to COVID, but I know there's an answer—I just need to get to it so I can take action right away.

"Do I simply enter my alpha level and ask the question, or should I be using a specific method for that type of communication?"

A 3-Step Solution

Here are our suggestions:

First analyze the problem. If you have learned how to enter the alpha level, then enter it and do some deepening. You can do some physical and mental relaxation, some countdowns, recall some of the Beneficial Statements, anything to help you relax.

You will be functioning at your center—the 10 cycles per second alpha brainwave frequency. That is the center of the normal brain frequency range (up to 20 cycles per second, where we function when we are using our eyesight and taking physical action).

Alpha is also the mid-brain area, the center of the brain itself.

Why Is Alpha Valuable?

Functioning at alpha puts you closer to the information and memories that can help you.

It is also the strongest and most stable part of the brain.

Mr. Silva's knowledge of electronics told him that the strongest electrical circuit is the one with the lowest impedance.

In the brain, that means the part of the brain with the fewest impediments to our ability to think and analyze information and come up with solutions to difficult problems.

More Information Available at Alpha

He proved his theory:

He would bring children into the laboratory and connect them to an electroencephalograph (EEG) and ask them questions. He might ask them how many ways they could think of to clean a car.

While at the 20 cycles beta level, they would have several ideas: wash it, wax it, clean the chrome.

Then he would guide them to the 10 cycles alpha level and ask them again. They would come up with more ideas: vacuum the inside, clean the tires and the windshield, etc.

While you are at the alpha level, think about the kind of things you can do that are helpful and useful. Even small things.

2nd Step: Take Action

Mental work is only part of the process. Physical action is also required.

Do some research online. I am sure that if you search for something like "ideas to earn money during the pandemic" you should find plenty of ideas. (Yep, I just checked . . . lots of ideas online.)

Anything that sounds like something you might do well, enter your level and check it out. Perhaps you will recall having done that kind of work before. It doesn't matter if you did it for pay, for free, for fun, the important things are: Did it provide benefits that somebody would pay for, and were you good at it?

A Personal Case Study

When I was "terminated" from my newspaper career (that's the only work I'd done my whole life), I didn't know what was going to happen.

I knew I could earn a little money by producing a printed program for the local speedway. "Quick printing" was new in 1975 and that was perfect for me. I got the program printed at Kopy Kat Printing.

The owner, Georgia Shane, asked if I'd like to do some layout work for her in exchange for the printing. That led to a job that lasted three and a half years.

During that time I was told by a couple of my best friends that I had to take the Silva Mind Control course.

Then my Silva instructor insisted that I should learn to teach the course (which I was totally unqualified for, in my humble opinion).

"Coincidences" Guided Me

My job at Kopy Kat Printing provided both the time and the money to learn all about this new field of psychorientology and how we can all learn to orient (control) our mind for greater success.

If I had still been working as a bureau chief for a big daily newspaper, that never would have happened.

So you never know where an idea might lead until you take action on it in the physical world.

3rd Step: Now You Qualify to Ask for Help

Now that you have done your due diligence, it is time to ask higher intelligence what you should be doing with your life.

Review the MentalVideo formula, and follow it exactly. Here's how:

At beta, with your eyes open, use visualization to create a MentalVideo of the problem.

I think of it like the evening news report on local television. They only have a very short time to do their report. And that is all it takes:

A few seconds to "picture" the problem, then some quick "camera shots" of the efforts you are making—the research you are doing, people you are talking to, etc.

Then close your eyes and review your problem video with your eyes closed.

Later when you are ready to go to sleep, enter your level and review the problem video. Then use your imagination to create a solution video.

Imagine yourself getting an opportunity and taking advantage of it. The more information you can provide to higher intelligence, the better able they will be to help you.

Comply with the Laws of Programming

Keep the Laws of Programming in mind, and that you are looking for "constructive and creative" work that at least two or more people will benefit from, something that will be the best for everybody concerned. Picture many people benefiting.

I have also found it best to concentrate on what I can do now— to strive for what is within my personal "possibility area"—and let higher intelligence guide me. The future has often turned out a lot different than I expected.

My friends who told me about Silva Mind Control also told me that I should be working at Silva headquarters, doing public relations.

I didn't take it seriously. That idea seemed much too far-fetched.

But now that I look back, it seems inevitable that I would wind up working here. And loving it.

Keep It Simple

Your videos can be short, shorter than what I am writing here.

The universal form of communication is visual. That is why we use a "MentalVideo." Other people may speak a different language and not understand our words, but everybody "gets the picture."

Then relax and go to sleep like you normally do, and take it for granted that your two videos will be delivered to your tutor on the other side while you sleep.

Look for Indications

Then allow three days for "indications" of how to proceed.

The "indications" are physical, often what people think of as "coincidences."

Somebody might say something, or you might hear a song that gives you an idea. You might read something, or see something.

Maybe an idea will come to you. If that happens, take action on it and "see" what happens.

How to Tell Fact from Fiction

Our thoughts and ideas could be our own fantasies, our hopes, our fears. Actions in the physical world are a much more reliable way to determine if we are getting guidance from higher intelligence.

You might get your indication when you wake up in the morning. Or later in the day. Or the second day, or the third day.

Ask for a "Clear" Indication

If you don't recognize any indications after three days, ask again. Make a MentalVideo that indicates you didn't see any indications, and ask for a "clear" indication of what to do.

If this sounds like a lot to think about, then "sleep on it" and read it over again tomorrow.

Things often make a lot more sense to me after I "sleep on them." It gives the brain time to organize the material, so that you will understand it better.

CHAPTER 6

Find Your Purpose in Life

Most highly successful people use the principles of the Mental-Video Technique without even knowing it. José Silva was one of them. From a very young age he was guided to develop skills that he would use later when he was conducting research into the mind and human potential.

An experience he had in 1949, when he had decided to end his research, guided him to a winning lottery ticket.

It paid him $10,000, which was about two years salary for the average person in 1949.

That experience persuaded him to continue his research.

He has told the story many times, about how he had a very strange dream with numbers surrounded by bright lights, and how a series of "coincidences" led him to the one store in all of Mexico that had the lottery ticket with those numbers.

Here is how he interpreted the experience:

As elated as I was, I looked this gift horse carefully in the mouth, and what I found was more valuable by far than the gift itself. It was the foundation for a solidly based conviction that my studies were worthwhile.

Somehow I had made contact with higher intelligence. Maybe I had made contact with it many times before and not known; this time I knew.

Consider the number of seemingly chance events that led to this:

In a moment of despair, I dreamed of a number in so startling a way—with the light—that I had to recall it.

Then a friend dropped in to invite me for coffee and, tired as I was, I accepted.

My wife overheard us and asked me to bring rubbing alcohol, which led me to the only store in Mexico where that particular ticket was on sale.

We have no objection to the word "coincidence." In fact, we attach special meaning to it:

When a series of events that is hard to explain leads to a constructive result, we call it a coincidence. When they lead to a destructive result, we call it an accident.

My lottery-winning dream convinced me of the existence of higher intelligence and of its ability to communicate with me.

That is why I say that a coincidence is God's way of showing His hand.

Understanding What Happened

Even though he didn't realize it, Mr. Silva was using the main elements of the MentalVideo Technique that he developed forty-eight years later:

- He went to sleep thinking about his problem and what to do about it.
- The next day he looked for objective (physical) indications of what to do.
- These coincidences directed him towards his life's mission, and he continued this work for the rest of his life.

In 1997 the MentalVideo Technique was revealed to him and he spent the last two years of his life teaching people how to use it.

My journey has been filled with coincidences too. Like José Silva said:

- I didn't get into this business by accident.
- I didn't get into it deliberately either.
- It was coincidences that put me here.

In Chapter 5 I told you how I found a job after being "terminated" from my newspaper career.

In Chapter 7 I'll tell you the rest of the story: how I was led to my life's purpose by going to sleep thinking about my problems and how to solve them.

CHAPTER 7

How I Was Guided to My Life's Purpose

In Chapter 5 I mentioned some of the coincidences that led me to take the Silva Mind Control Course. Now let me tell you about a strange coincidence that led me to the work that I have been doing for the last forty-five years:

In 1975, I was unemployed for most of the year. I had been abruptly terminated from my newspaper career and spent most of the year living on unemployment. I was really burned out. I didn't know what to do. I began working part-time in a small family-owned quick printing shop that had done some printing for me.

One day I learned that a couple of friends of mine, Al and Vera Christensen, had moved back to Florida. They had recently taken the Silva Mind Control course. I went to visit them and they told me, "Ed, you've got to go take this course. It is the best thing you can do to help your weightlifting."

I went to the introductory lecture and heard all this talk about ESP. Nobody believed in ESP back in 1975. Well, very few people. Even those who did believe didn't see any value in it.

But I thought: "I've got nothing better to do. I'll go enjoy myself for a couple of weekends, have a few laughs, probably learn a little something, and then get my refund, so I won't be out any money."

Needless to say, it worked.

At the start of the course I didn't believe in psychics.

The following weekend I was functioning as a psychic.

I still had no idea what kind of job to look for or what to do with the rest of my life, so my instructor offered a suggestion. "You ought to start teaching the course."

I said, "Come on, I'm not a talker. I'm a writer." Everybody laughs when I say that. Well, I'm not a public talker. I didn't get up in public and talk to people. I'm a writer.

My instructor had a great voice. He was British and had a wonderful English accent. He was a fabulous orator, and taught oratory. I recall thinking that I would love to do what he was doing, but there was no way I could be a lecturer for Silva.

I got involved in a local graduate group, repeated the course, and was practicing and was getting some impressive results. Wonderful things were beginning to happen in my life.

I thought, "Well, even if I don't ever teach it, if I study and learn how to teach it, at least I will learn more about it." So I came up with an idea to see if higher intelligence wanted me to do this. Oh, wait, I don't know why I thought it was *my* idea, so let me say it differently: An idea came to me:

There was a Silva graduate named Bill Guggenheim who was recording all the classes and giving the recordings to Silva students for free. Bill didn't need to work, so he used his time and the money he had inherited to carry on the family tradition and do whatever he could to solve problems and help people.

I devised a small test. I told my instructor, "All right, I'll study to become an instructor on one condition: Get me a set of recordings of the class that I took. My first class."

He asked Bill for a set of the tapes.

Bill said he had given out the last set, and that he was involved in something else and didn't have time to make any more.

I figured, okay, I don't have to become an instructor.

A couple of days later when I got home from the print shop I walked down to my mailbox, and in it was a package.

I wasn't expecting any packages.

I looked at the return address:

It was from Bill Guggenheim in Orlando, and I knew what was in it.

My first thought was, "Darn, now I'm going to have to become a Silva instructor!"

When I opened the package, there were a dozen audio cassette tapes, so I began the journey I am still on forty-eight years later.

I thanked Bill, and then twenty-one years later, after I'd been working for José Silva at Silva headquarters in Laredo, Texas, for fifteen years, I called Bill and thanked him again. He was excited about research he had started in 1988 into "After Death Communication," which led to his book *Hello from Heaven!*, which was published in 1996 by Bantam Books.

How Did That Coincidence Come About?

Looking back, now I understand how it happened:

I was going to the alpha level at night and going to sleep from my level. When you do that, the message gets through to higher intelligence, and your tutor arranges coincidences to guide you to do what they want you to do. I didn't know it at the time, but that's what was happening to me.

The more I learned about José Silva, the more I learned that similar things had happened to him his entire life. His intuition and the guidance from higher intelligence helped him to make the correct decisions throughout his life.

You already know *more* about how to get guidance from higher intelligence to help you make the correct decisions in every area of your life than I knew, more than José Silva knew, back in 1975.

Chapter 3 explains how you can apply the Mental Video Technique tonight. You will be communicating with higher intelligence. You will get guidance to help you make better decisions in every area of your life.

Imagine the benefits.

Benefits to health, to make the correct decisions. How many times have you gone to the doctor and he says, "Oh, you'll be over this in a few days," or how many times have you put off going to the doctor and paid a penalty for it? You can make the right decisions when you have your intuition helping you.

What about relationships? I heard somewhere that there are more divorces than there are marriages now. That's an indication that we're making wrong choices. It takes too many attempts to finally find the right one. Wouldn't it be better to make that right choice the first time?

When you have a family, children, there are so many decisions to make that are going to affect them for the rest of their lives. Can you give them more freedom without them getting into trouble? If you are a little more restrictive with them, will they resent you for that and rebel and get into trouble? The right decisions are so important.

What about your career, your job: How many people are in jobs they hate, that they get no satisfaction from, where they don't feel like they're making any contribution or doing anything to improve conditions here on the planet? You may or may not love your work. When you are doing the right work that you are sent here to do, at least you should have the sense of satisfaction of knowing that you're doing some good, that you're accomplishing something.

What area of your life would you use it first? What area do you have decisions pending right now that you would like to use your intuition to detect more information, to have more information to base your decision on?

You can get started tonight.

CHAPTER 8

The Silva Way to World Peace

For forty years people worldwide feared that the cold war would erupt into a nuclear war and destroy all life on planet Earth.

Back in 1986 José Silva's brother Juan, our Director of Foreign Countries, had made a trip around the world visiting Silva Method national directors. He literally circled the globe and ended up back in Laredo. He was having trouble sleeping when he got back, due to jet lag, so he watched some live news on television.

He told me about it the next morning:

He said he was watching a live picture of U.S. President Ronald Reagan and Soviet Union Premier Mikhail Gorbachev at their meeting in Reykjavik, Iceland. "I didn't have to imagine what they were doing or what their surroundings were like," he said. "I could see them on live television."

He realized that would be a great time to program them, so he did.

Juan was a great negotiator; he managed all of our foreign operations. He often had to deal with difficult situations, and he did it very well.

I didn't ask him how he programmed, but I am sure that he used his skill and experience to project ideas mentally to the two world leaders, to persuade them to work toward peace, to be honest with each other, to trust each other.

When he was finished, he went to bed with that project on his mind.

They didn't reach an agreement to eliminate all nuclear weapons, which they had wanted to do, but the meeting did lead to the first treaty to cut strategic nuclear arms significantly, and they promised to work together on other mutually beneficial projects.

A couple of years later I watched live pictures on television as the Berlin Wall was torn down.

Many diplomats and experts consider the Reykjavik summit a turning point in the Cold War.

For forty years the world had lived in fear of total destruction by nuclear war. Schoolchildren were taught to "duck and cover" and hide under their desks in the event of a nuclear attack. Homeowners built bomb shelters and stocked them with food, water, and other supplies, and debated whether they would let their neighbors join them. The United States and Russia spent billions of dollars and rubles on nuclear weapons they never used.

In late 1991 the Soviet Union itself dissolved into its component republics. With stunning speed, the Iron Curtain was lifted and the cold war came to an end.

On Juan's next trip to Germany, he visited the Berlin Wall— the rubble that was left—and he brought back some of the stones that had once been part of the wall. I asked him for one of the little pieces of the wall, and I still have it today, a reminder about what is possible if only more people will use the faculties that higher intelligence gave us.

There is no way to prove that Juan influenced events. But when you keep seeing coincidences, it begins to seem pretty natural.

You may have already noticed that what he did paralleled the steps in the MentalVideo: he visualized the problem, then imagined the solution, and went bed with a strong desire for the solution to be materialized.

That's why we believe in the Silva courses. It was always the dream that José and Juan Silva had.

They believed we can do far more than just continue to deal with problems.

We can bring peace to the planet.

CHAPTER 9

How to Ask for Things for Yourself

"How much help you get, from higher intelligence, depends on how big your plans are. The bigger your plans are—meaning: how many people will benefit—the more help you will qualify for."

--JOSÉ SILVA

When we are doing what we were sent here to do, then we can ask for help from higher intelligence and get it, to take care of our own problems and our own needs.

It is not a matter of reward and punishment, but of encouraging us to do what we were sent here to do. Higher intelligence is not going to reward us or encourage us to do things that we should not be doing.

But when we are doing what we were sent here to do—correct problems, relieve suffering, and improve living conditions on the planet—then we can ask for whatever we need and we will get it.

We need to let higher intelligence know what our needs are, just as we need to let them know about problems that we need guidance and help with in order to correct them.

We need two-way communication in order to be effective:

We are like fingers on the hand of God—we can detect information here in the physical world and communicate it back to higher intelligence in the spiritual (non-physical) dimension, just as your fingers can detect information and transmit that information to your brain.

Then higher intelligence will send information back to us via "coincidences" so we can do the work, just as your fingers receive signals from the brain through the motor nerves, and can do what needs to be done.

Higher intelligence (God) is spiritual, not physical. The only way that higher intelligence can find out what is going on in the physical world is through us. That is why we were created.

We are part of the hierarchy of intelligences that we call higher intelligence. We need to report on problems in order to help us correct the problems. We need to report on what we need in order to continue to carry out our mission.

Can I Ask for Luxury Items?

José Silva was asked a question during instructor training in 1995, if higher intelligence will help us if we program to get a Rolls-Royce. Here is his answer, transcribed from the recording:

You are asking a good question. He's asking for a Rolls-Royce. This is in the possibility area.

But you see, we were not sent ... and we're not going to get help from the other side ... when we want something like this only for me.

But if I say, "I want this vehicle, that *we* can use"—*we*, not just *me*—because there is a need for something like this, and it's within the possibility area, and I don't have the means, I may then get the other side to help me.

Now the other side will only help me when I am asking for something that is needed to improve conditions on planet Earth.

Like we said, they are not going to help me if I want another million dollars when I already have a million dollars, when I want a Rolls-Royce when I have a Rolls-Royce already. That I want a girlfriend when I already have a wife. Some people ask for something like this.

They are not going to help you. You are on your own.

If you make a mistake, you are going to suffer for it. You are on your own. You don't get help from the other side.

You only get help from the other side when your intentions are that whatever you are doing is to help improve conditions on the planet for more than yourself, not just yourself.

If you only consider *me, me, me*, you have to do it on your own. If it is for *us*, then you get help, if whatever you do is going to help more than you.

The more you are going to help, the more help you get for it.

We always say:

Don't ever ask for more than what you need, but *do* ask for *no less* than what you need.

So what your needs will be depends on how big your plans are. That's what your needs will be.

Unexpected Successes

José Silva's nephew Sam Gonzalez was one of the first to sign up to teach the newest course, the Silva UltraMind ESP System. It was a natural for him, because he had observed something very similar to the MentalVideo.

Sam liked to program mentally to correct problems at night just before going to sleep. He had a lot of success doing that.

He also realized that he had a lot of success even when he didn't actually program to solve the problem.

"Sometimes graduates ask me to work on problems for them," Sam said, "and I intend to, but fall asleep first. But somehow it often works anyway and the problem is solved."

Now we know what was happening.

When he went to sleep:

• He knew about the problem.
• He knew the desired solution.
• He had a desire to help manifest the solution.
• He had confidence in his ability because he had been using his mind to solve problems since he was young.

"Even if you forget to program, you can still get results," he said.

It was experiences like these that helped José Silva understand how coincidences worked and where they came from. Then he used his vast experience in researching the mind and human potential to develop a simple method that we can all use to learn how to ask for help from higher intelligence and get the guidance and help we need.

Once you see it working for you, you can use your successful experiences to help you shorten the ritual, and even to develop the ability to ask for help and get it during the day when necessary.

A Miracle Success We Take for Granted Today

I had a similar experience almost twenty years before José Silva created the MentalVideo Technique.

My problem was that the air conditioning was broken in the storefront I had leased in a building in Cocoa Beach, Florida. It needed a new compressor.

It was spring and the weather was heating up.

There was no compressor anywhere in Florida that would fit this air conditioner, so the technician had ordered one from out of state.

It was on the way when truck drivers decided to boycott Florida because state troopers began ticketing them for driving more than fifty-five miles per hour. That was costing the truck drivers a lot of money.

So the compressor we needed was in a truck parked just north of the state line, along with thousands of other trucks.

The air conditioning technician had assured me on Thursday afternoon that "I have searched everywhere and there is no compressor anywhere in the state of Florida that will work with your air conditioner." This was one day before class started.

On Thursday night, I was doing my regular programming before going to sleep when I suddenly realized I had never programmed mentally for the air conditioner to be fixed. There hadn't been any problem; everything was going according to plan, until the truckers' boycott.

So I decided to program, even though the technician had assured me the situation was hopeless. I used a technique from José Silva's first course, the Mirror of the Mind technique:

First you enter the alpha level and project a mental image of the problem into an imaginary mirror.

Then erase the problem image and use your imagination to create an image of the solution.

It took less than a minute to do the programming. Then I finished the other programming I had planned to do that night, and went to sleep.

At 8 a.m. the phone rang. It was the air conditioning technician. The first thing I said was: "What time do you want me to meet you there?"

"Um . . . I have the compressor we need. . . ."

I spoke up quickly: "I thought that was probably why you were calling. Can I meet you at the building in an hour?"

"That will be perfect," he replied.

He completed the installation and it was working that afternoon. Problem solved.

I never did ask him where he found the compressor, or where it came from.

The way I used the Mirror of the Mind technique paralleled the MentalVideo formula:

I had been thinking about the problem at the outer conscious level, at the beta brainwave level.

I had been doing everything I could to solve the problem but had encountered unexpected obstacles that were beyond my control.

That night, I used the best technique that was available at the time and visualized the problem: the hot meeting room that would be a less-than-ideal learning environment.

Then I imagined the solution—a cool meeting room, filled with people who were excited and happy to be learning life-changing techniques for solving problems.

I also imagined what it would take to manifest this solution: we needed to get a compressor.

I thought about everything that contained life: the truck drivers who were parked just north of the Florida border and also the air conditioning repairman and the people he had talked to in an effort to get the compressor we needed.

I was using my ESP—psychic ability—to communicate the situation to higher intelligence with a strong desire for a solution that would be the best for everybody concerned.

I complied with all of the Laws of Programming.

I went to sleep, which allowed the project to be transferred to higher intelligence when I was in deep sleep, at the delta brainwave level.

CHAPTER 10

How to Improve Your Quality of Life

William James said: "The deepest principle in human nature is the craving to be appreciated." He didn't speak, mind you, of the "wish" or the "desire" or the "longing" to be appreciated. He said the "craving" to be appreciated.

—QUOTED FROM DALE CARNEGIE'S BOOK,
HOW TO WIN FRIENDS AND INFLUENCE PEOPLE

Most people, when they talk about "quality of life," are talking about more than financial well-being.

Recent surveys reveal that only 34 percent of all global workers describe themselves as "thriving." Young people are the most frustrated, with only 31 percent expressing satisfaction with their quality of life.

Researchers have discovered that young people are avoiding work, experiencing burnout, and encountering mental health issues because they are not finding the inspiration and opportunities they crave.

They want to do something important, something to make a difference.

The MentalVideo can certainly help you:

- Find a job you love
- Do work that benefits many people
- Succeed at your job
- Get paid for doing the work you love
- Accomplish beneficial things
- Improve living conditions on the planet
- Make a difference

The Laws of Programming can help you with all of that, especially the first one: "Do unto others only what you want others to do unto you."

José Silva added, "If you don't want it done to you, then don't do it to others."

You can review the Laws of Programming in Chapter 3.

Doing Work You Can See

Many years ago I became friends with a carpenter who was building a custom-made desk for me. He hadn't always been a carpenter. He used to be an insurance salesman. He told me that he made a lot more money selling insurance, but that was the only benefit he got. He didn't see people benefiting from his work.

He definitely saw how happy I was with the desk he made for me. It was a modular design so that when I moved to a new location I could just load each module into a truck or trailer, and put the modules back together again when I got to my destination.

He was proud of how beautiful the desk was. To him, that was worth more than the extra money he had made when he was selling insurance. Maybe that is why so many sales organizations give trophies and plaques to their top salespeople, and take them on luxury cruises—that gives them something they can see.

José Silva was a great salesman, and he always made sure he could see the benefits of his work, whether it was shining shoes as a six-year-old child, refurbishing radios so that people who couldn't afford a new radio could still get one, or teaching Silva Mind Control with all of the benefits that it provided to people.

The Importance of Friends

Friends are important to our quality of life. The MentalVideo can help you find them, and to know how to approach them, what to share with them, how to support them.

Remember to lay the groundwork first:

- Look for opportunities to meet new people.
- Ask people about themselves.
- Encourage them.

Note: There are other mental tools you can use to solve problems. You learn to develop and use your natural God-given ESP in the Silva UltraMind Systems ESP training. The Appendix has information about other Silva books, courses, and workshops you can use.

CHAPTER 11

Solving Life's Biggest Problems

José Silva wondered, "If God is all powerful, then why did He create us? I was sent by somebody who had the power to send me, so what is my purpose?"

His research, his observations, and his life experience all convinced him that our purpose is to correct problems and improve living conditions on the planet.

If higher intelligence sent us here to do a job, do you think they would just leave us on our own, without any guidance or feedback?

Have you ever had a boss who said, "Just go do the job and don't bother me with it"? Of course not.

Most employers want to know what you're doing and how you're doing it. Supervisors want to know what you're doing. They're going to recommend ways to improve. They're going to use insight that you don't have.

They go to their meetings and they know more about what the company's objectives are. They know more about problems that other people have had. They can use that information to guide you to do your job more effectively.

Do you think that higher intelligence isn't going to do that with us? Do you think they just sent us here and are going to leave us on our own? No chance. They are there to help us.

José Silva got very dramatic confirmation of the validity of these concepts in two very different cases. Here is what happened, in his own words:

Ask for Help When You Need It

One day as I was in my office a friend came to see me. He told me that his brother, who was a city official, was going to die that night.

"But I talked with your brother two days ago," I said.

"That night," my friend told me, "he felt very bad and went to the hospital. They found that his kidneys had some kind of infection and had stopped functioning. The hospital could not get a dialysis machine."

There was a dialysis machine in a San Antonio hospital, he told me, but it was being used on a patient. In those years, only a few hospitals had dialysis equipment. Meanwhile, our sick man had lapsed into a coma due to urea poisoning in his brain.

As soon as my friend left the office, I went to the hospital to see his brother. I got there very quickly since the hospital is only six blocks from my office.

When I got to the room of the sick official, his mother and sister were present. His mother told me that the doctors had tried all day to bring her son out of the coma, but had failed. Doctors had given them little hope that he would live.

I then said, "Excuse me, I will now pray for him."

I stood next to the bed and went into my clairvoyant level. Then I made believe someone, somehow was listening to what I was saying and picturing mentally:

"This man is thirty-four years old. He has a big, strong body and there is much work to be done on this planet. I don't believe it is justified that because his kidneys stopped functioning, he has to go. All his other organs, glands, and systems are young and functioning well. Why not let us get the kidneys to function again?"

As I was identifying the problem and the solution in my mind, our sick official sat up in bed, looked at me with the eyes of a somnambulist (a sleepwalker), the whites of the eyes now turned yellowish with the urea poisoning, recognized me, and said,

"Hi, José, what are you doing here?"

I answered, "What are you doing here?"

He responded, "Where am I?"

"You are in the right place," I answered. "Close your eyes, go back to sleep, and everything is going to be all right."

He closed his eyes, fell back on the pillow, and appeared to go back into a coma.

The mother told her daughter to run and get the doctor and tell him what had happened.

Two hours later, the sick official started to pass urine, his kidneys started to function normally, and at this writing he is still alive.

It seemed as though higher intelligence didn't know about it, like the feedback mechanism failed to report back. I was the feedback mechanism that reported the problem to the other side so they could take action.

The nuns at the hospital named the city official "The Miracle Kid." He never remembered having talked to me, even after his mother told him what had happened.

Another Dramatic Case

Another time we used this concept was for a man, eighty-six years old, who had been in a coma for forty-five days. He wouldn't die. He was like a living vegetable.

I entered my clairvoyant level and reported the situation to higher intelligence in this manner:

"If this man is supposed to stay, we are going to see a change within seventy-two hours, an improvement, and we'll consider it our obligation to continue to work with this individual at least once every seventy-two hours until he is on his feet again.

"If not, then we will assume that it is time for him to move on and be assigned somewhere else."

Then, as we were there working with him, in less than a minute he passed.

It was like he had been forgotten here, for some reason. We were right there, working on that case, and higher intelligence took care of it right then.

My Analysis of These Experiences

Our concept is that the highest of all intelligence can do anything, but we need to play our role, so that higher intelligence can become aware of what's going on.

We are physical extensions and sensing mechanisms and feedback systems of the Creator.

But like the brain needs the fingers to sense information, we are the fingers and extensions of our Creator so we can sense information and relay it back to higher intelligence.

If something is beyond repair, you can't help them. If it's not beyond repair, then you can help them.

You can apply this approach to any kind of problem, family relations, business, any kind of problem where people are suffering.

If people are suffering then you have a good reason to intercede to solve the problem, because we are problem solvers. That's our obligation.

You can expect to see something happen within seventy-two hours.

Natural Abortion

There is something else that we can think about when it comes to making the most difficult decisions.

Here in the United States, we're pretty much evenly divided over the abortion issue: Should we or shouldn't we?

We don't have to make every decision ourselves. We can get help from higher intelligence. Here is a story I heard about a group of people who were asked what advice they would give in this situation.

A woman has tuberculosis. The father has syphilis. Together, they have four children. The first was born blind. The second was stillborn. The third child was deaf and dumb. The fourth was born with tuberculosis. They're now pregnant with their fifth child. They come to you for guidance. They are considering an abortion.

They don't know whether to do that or not. They will accept your recommendation. What would you recommend?

Now, according to the story, the people discussed it and the majority said:

"Under those circumstances, we would recommend an abortion."

"Congratulations," the group leader said, "you have just taken the life of Beethoven."

That would have deprived humanity of one of history's greatest musical geniuses.

That's a good story as far as it goes. Let's turn it around and look at the other side of it:

Suppose they had been able to determine that the fetus was defective. Should they have gone ahead with the birth anyway? If they did, then this great musical genius, Beethoven, would be trapped in a body that was unable to express that tremendous talent and art that he brought to the planet.

There could be physical problems that prevent him from making music and then what? Imagine what torture that would be for him. We would be deprived of that music for a lifetime, have to wait until that soul could go and come again, if it does. I'm not sure if it does or if it doesn't. Research is inconclusive on that.

Does that mean that if we know the fetus is defective and the child will not be able to produce and perform, does that mean we should do an abortion so that the soul will have an opportunity to incarnate in a healthy body?

Maybe.

If we take that as an absolute, we could deprive the world of a Helen Keller. Helen had an illness that left her deaf and blind at the age of nineteen months. She was a very troubled child, as you would expect. How frustrating her disability must have been, especially when you have the creative spark that Helen Keller had.

When Helen was six years old a young woman named Anne Sullivan began communicating with her through touch, and that made all the difference:

With Anne Sullivan's help Helen Keller learned to write and to talk. She wrote books and she gave lectures and she inspired millions of people.

If we abort a fetus simply because it's defective, that might be just as bad.

What do we do?

Let's call on higher intelligence. Let higher intelligence make the decision.

Guidance from a Higher Power

Medical science is often able to tell if a pregnancy is viable or not, or if there is the potential for serious complications.

Trained medical clairvoyants can detect information, including information that cannot be obtained through physical means. José Silva developed a "correlation" technique that virtually eliminates any chance of error.

Then they can alert higher intelligence of the situation so that, if appropriate, higher intelligence can cause a natural abortion if a defective conception has been detected and if God so desires.

If so, then the soul can move on to another experience that will be more beneficial. Everyone benefits, and nobody is going against God or doing something that God doesn't approve of.

We are not at the top. Anybody who comes back and says we have to make the choice, we have to say, "Never have an abortion," or we have to say, "Abort a defective fetus." Anybody who insists that we do it their way is trying to play God, aren't they?

If we have the ability to obtain guidance from higher intelligence, shouldn't we do so?

I hope that all people—whether they are pro-life or pro-choice—can agree to be pro-God and call on higher intelligence and give God an opportunity to help make that decision.

CHAPTER 12

Examples of Creative and Unexpected Coincidences

Whether you call it a MentalVideo or bedtime prayers or help from The Almighty or synchronicity or serendipity or something else, many of the luckiest people admit that "coincidences" helped them.

Here are some examples of how coincidences have helped solve all kinds of problems and improved the lives of individuals from all walks of life.

Finds Shelter from the Storm for His Family

On June 20, 2022, a man who had recently completed the Silva training, wrote and told us that he was using the MentalVideo Technique to find a place to stay and to work through his problems.

"Things won't be easy to work through," he said, "but I'm confident that I have the strength and peace of mind to make it through." Ten days later he sent us this inspiring message:

A quick update for you! I have found a place to stay for the moment to get me out of the hotel room. Quite miraculously in fact.

Back in December we experienced three different tornadoes in the area that destroyed a lot of housing in an already tight market. As I had been looking for a place, nothing was available or even a chance to have an opening until September, except property well outside my price range. More expensive than staying in a hotel room!

So one day I went driving in an area I would like to stay in and saw a small sign in front of a property that wasn't listed anywhere I had looked. I put it on my list to call but didn't get back to it for a few days while running down other leads.

By the time I did call the following week the owner answered and said he wasn't sure how I came across it as he had taken the sign down because he had decided to leave the place empty for the time being. He had someone move in for a week that didn't work out and had to ask them to leave within a few days.

He invited me to come view the property and after talking for a bit said he would like to help me out and I moved in the next week!

While I have other things to work through, this is a first step in putting things together! Thank you for making this program available!

Losing One Job Led to a Better Job

Have you ever gotten a "lucky break" that got you out of a jam? Or directed you toward a great opportunity?

Dusty Baker saw a disappointment turn into an opportunity that led to a World Series championship.

He already had a great job managing the Washington Nationals major league baseball team. But they didn't renew his contract.

His son consoled him: "Maybe there's something better for you out there."

Sure enough, when the Houston Astros heard that he was available, they offered him a job as manager. He was the perfect person:

"I'd be going against what I was destined to do if I did anything else at this point in time," he said. "I prayed on it and my answer was: 'Hey, man, get your butt back out there and manage again.'"

His integrity, compassion, and enthusiasm—along with his baseball skills—helped restore the team's reputation after a major cheating scandal, and he led them to the 2022 World Series championship.

We can't all win a World Series, but we can all have "lucky breaks" in our own personal and professional lives.

A Coincidence Helps Many People

Several years ago a man named Brian Schnabel contacted us with a question:

"Since the Silva programs rely so much on visualization, will they work for someone who has been blind all his life?"

Of all the Silva websites he could have contacted, he wrote to the one that was being managed by someone whose best friend in college was blind.

That was the first in a series of coincidences that guided both of us to develop abilities we didn't know we had. This helped a lot of other people along the way, and is continuing to help even more.

My college friend introduced me to a lot of blind students, and they would often ask me if they could touch my face. They would touch it very gently with their hands for a few seconds so they would know what I looked like.

We advised Brian to use his hands to help him "see" what something looks like, and that advice helped him get outstanding results with the coursework.

It has also helped sighted people to improve their mental images.

We tell people that "your mind can help your body do what it needs to do, and your body can help your mind do what it needs to do." You can learn more about using your hands to improve your visualization in Chapter 17.

A Safe Place to Live for Her and Her Family

Here is an impressive success that a lady named Shakeenah Kedem Fentis sent to us, exactly the way she wrote it:

In the year of 2011, my youth and I were still somewhat displaced from our departure a year prior, from an abusive family life. We had landed in a quaint town called Eureka Springs, located in the Ozarks of the state of Arkansas.

By this time, we had already stayed at a woman's shelter briefly, and several private homes of individuals willing to help us out. Then I worked out a deal with a real estate company to rent a beautiful old home that they had up for sale, until they had a buyer under contract. Due to the challenging rental situation in the area, I was smart enough to ask for forty-five days instead of thirty days to move out when that time came.

A few months passed, and someone decided to buy the house. I began searching for a house to rent and finding an affordable one was extremely difficult. I was able to find a house that was big enough, but that I was unsure of due to several factors. Then I heard briefly about another space that I could afford, but the description did not sound appealing or practical.

Therefore, I decided to use one of the tools I had learned from studying José Silva's teachings regarding using our gifts of intuition to get answers from our Higher Self / Higher Intelligence.

Upon preparing to go to sleep, I told my mind that I needed to have a dream that revealed if I should go for the big house or not. I was nearing the deadline and was under lots of pressure.

I woke up the next morning with nothing but a confusing recollection of bits and pieces of the dream(s) I had that night. Then I recalled that I need to be REALLY clear and specific with my command before falling asleep and decided to try it again that following evening. I told myself that I want to have a dream that CLEARLY tells me if I should rent this house that I looked at already, and I included the street.

I am glad that I had patience with myself and the process because the next morning I woke up not even remembering much of a dream but instead with a loud and clear voice in my head that said "MISTAKE." Ha! That Creative Energy got straight to the point!

I was overwhelmed with gratitude for HIGHER INTELLI-GENCE speaking to me through my inner conscious mind and responding to my request for assistance!

I looked at the new option and it turned out to be exactly what I needed. It also turned out to be on a street that I had previously dreamed about living on.

Also, while it was a basement apartment, the owner of the house offered me the upstairs main part of the house with a beautiful screened-in balcony overlooking the wooded backyard once the upstairs neighbors moved out.

My mother moved to the same town to be with me and her grandchildren: She took the basement apartment, and we moved upstairs.

To me it was the most beautiful house on the block, and I am forever grateful for my stay there.

How the MentalVideo Helped Launch a New Business

Here is an experience that helped me land the biggest "business deal" of my life.

In 1975 I took the Silva Mind Control course to see if it would help my weightlifting. By the end of the course I had become much more interested in learning to use more of my mind, and that is what I have focused on ever since.

When I came to work at Silva headquarters six years later, I learned that José Silva has been a professional athlete, a boxer. He was still staying in shape: He had a barbell set in his bedroom, and whenever he wasn't traveling and presenting classes he would get his cardio conditioning by "walking the mall" with his wife, Paula.

So I asked him for a technique that could help me lift heavier weights. It only took him a few minutes to design both the Mental Rehearsal Technique and the Mental Coach for motivation.

He also modified the first Beneficial Statement in the Silva Mind Control course. The original reads: "My increasing mental faculties are for serving humanity better." He changed it to something for young athletes: "My increasing strength and fitness are so I can serve as a role model for others."

I started using those techniques. I made audio recordings of the instructions and wrote up a short booklet, all with his help and approval.

Then we talked business.

He was willing to produce an audio cassette tape kit and sell it. I asked if he would allow me to produce it and sell it and pay him a royalty for all the sales I made.

He had not let anyone do that before. A couple of people who were helping him when he was conducting his research had stolen his research notes and started their own company. Their company failed, and he was very cautious after that.

But he said he would consider letting me produce and market the product, and told me to draw up a contract.

That contract must have been about six or eight pages. After he read through it, he told me, "That's too long. We need a one-page contract."

I replied, "That sounds like a 'Letter of Agreement.' I'll work on it."

A couple of days later I gave it to him to review.

I waited for his suggestions. And waited. A week went by and he didn't mention it. I finally decided I should say something and find out where we stood and what else he wanted.

So that night after I got in bed, I went to my level—the alpha level—which you can learn to do in Chapter 16 if you don't already know, and I "mentally rehearsed" exactly what I would say to him the next day:

"Are you ready to sign the Agreement?"

I rehearsed it over and over, and imagined that I was happy with his reply.

"Are you ready to sign the agreement?"

When I saw him in the office the next day, I walked over to ask him if he was ready to sign the agreement and I heard myself say:

"Are you ready for me to sign the agreement?"

"Me?!" I thought: *his* signature is the one that counts.

Even though I was alarmed that I didn't say what I had programmed myself to say, I also realized that asking if *he* was ready to sign it was much better: It was a way of showing him that I was ready, willing, and able to do whatever he wanted me to do.

His reaction surprised me too. He replied immediately: "Yes, where is it? Do you have it?"

"I gave it to you—is it in your office?"

"Yes," he said as he turned and quickly started down the hall. "Let's go get it."

I hurried along behind him. He found the agreement and signed it, and I signed it, and the Silva Star Athlete program was born.

If you already know how to use the MentalVideo Technique, as explained in Chapter 3, then you will see the similarities and how I:

- had been thinking about it at the outer conscious level,
- thought about the problem and the solution at the alpha level,

- went to sleep with a desire to do what was best for everybody concerned,
- and a lot of people benefited.

Once he had taken that first step and let me publish a little audio cassette tape set, he authorized Burt Goldman, one of the top Silva lecturers, to develop and present his Silva Supermind seminar. Local Silva lecturers would sponsor Burt, hundreds of people would attend, and everybody benefited.

Mr. Silva slowly allowed other top Silva lecturers to use some of the Silva techniques to develop and present their own seminars, and eventually he started letting any Silva lecturers with a certain amount of experience present the Silva Graduate Seminar.

Higher Intelligence Is Very Creative

When I am working on a book, I tend to write a chapter a day. At night, before I go to bed, I review what I have already written and think about what comes next. I think about the words I plan to use, and how to arrange those words to make it easy for you to read them and understand them.

The next day when I am sitting at the keyboard, I have something in mind, I start typing, and something better appears on the screen. It is still on-topic; it is just a better way to say it. Or a better example than the one I had in mind.

Silva UltraMind graduate Collayne Mills has a similar experience. She says that when she is painting or writing her poem stories for six year olds, "I just show up for work."

It is similar for Robert B. Stone, who co-authored several books with José Silva. When he needs information for a book he is writing, it shows up without him searching for it. Maybe a magazine that arrives in the mail that day has an article with the information he needs.

As he said, "Maybe creativity is the expression of our spirituality."

CHAPTER 13

How Higher Intelligence Helped Solve a Texas Murder

by José Silva

In 1967 we had started to teach on a regular basis in a certain city in Texas when we became aware that the chairman of the department of psychology of the local college (it is now a university) was interested in bringing his psychology class to observe our work and comment on it. This they did.

Later, a woman who worked as a janitor at the college was murdered in a laboratory at the college, and after several months of investigation, the police had no clues to go on.

One Monday morning, after we had finished training a group and were packing to move on to another city to train another group, two gentlemen came to talk to us. They were in charge of the detective division of the police department in that city.

These men had been told by the head of the department of psychology that perhaps we could help in finding clues that they could use in their investigation. The officers wanted to know if this was possible.

I said, "Yes, it is. A clairvoyant, from their clairvoyant level, can regress in time and can know how the person was killed and can describe the murderer. Sometimes the progress is easier when we have a piece of clothing from either the victim or the murderer," I explained. "The clairvoyant just holds the piece of clothing in his hand while getting the information."

The officers asked, "Will you do it for us?"

"No," I replied.

They wanted to know why, and I said, "Because we have sworn that we will never use our system to hurt anybody under any circumstances. If I help you to capture him, you are going to hurt him and that would be our using our system for hurting a human being."

The officers then said, "We feel it is your obligation toward society as much as it is ours to capture this criminal and keep them from hurting others. Besides, this person may be sick and in need of help himself. If this is the case, he will be sent to a hospital for treatment and that would stop him from hurting others."

"I understand what you are saying," I replied, "but that is your duty, to capture criminals, and our duty is to train people to develop clairvoyance. How you use it depends on your duties."

The police officers then said, "You mean to tell us that you would teach us clairvoyance so then we, ourselves, could use clairvoyance to capture criminals?"

I answered, "What you do with it is up to you."

"Well, train us," they said. "How much will it cost?"

I said, "For you to use it for that purpose, we will do it free of charge."

"We are ready, then," they answered quickly.

I then said, "We will be back one month from today to teach another group. You can then be trained."

They said, "We would like to be trained now."

I said, "Right now, that is impossible. If you had come this past weekend, you would have been trained in the first part of the training. There are four parts to the total training, and in this city we teach a part each month. In other cities, we start on a Monday night and teach every weeknight and all day Saturday and Sunday and that way we complete the full training in seven days. But the way we do it in this city, it would take four months."

"We can't wait that long," the officers answered. "Is there any other way of doing it?"

I said, "Yes, by following us around from city to city until you complete your training."

They said they could not do that either. They were about to leave when one said, "Is there any other way that you could help us?"

I said, "Yes."

They wanted to know how.

"By presenting the case to high intelligence," I said.

At that point, they looked at each other. I could detect a confused appearance on their faces, and one said, "You mean like God?"

I said, "Yes."

Again they looked at each other, still appearing confused. Then one said, "And how long do we have to wait for that?"

"Three days," I said.

Both officers said at the same time, "Three days?"

I said, "Yes, three days."

They appeared more confused than ever, and with a tone in their voices as though they were talking to a crank or a loony, they then said, "Let us think about it and we will let you know later. All right?"

I said that was all right, and they departed.

We kept on going and meeting our obligations to continue training other groups in other cities.

Seeking Help from Higher Intelligence

One month later we returned on a Monday to the city where the murder had taken place. In our hotel mailbox was a large envelope with pictures of the murdered person in the university laboratory, and a campus map indicating the building where the murder had taken place.

Along with the pictures and the map was a note saying, "Please do whatever you can to help us."

Although there were no signatures on the note, we knew where it came from.

That night, I presented the case to high intelligence.

Indications of Success

That same night, or early in the morning of the following day, someone entered the office of one of the professors at the college. Investigators theorized it was to find answers to test questions.

A detective was assigned to watch the building the next night to see if that individual would enter again. Sure enough the individual entered the same office again.

When the detective tried to capture him, the suspect escaped on a bicycle, through the buildings and pathways. He had a car parked close by, and when he reached his car he threw the bicycle in the trunk and fled in the car. Officers who were patrolling in police cars were notified by radio and gave chase. They captured the fugitive at the edge of town.

This person had on him a master key that he had used to enter the professor's office. The master key had belonged to the janitor woman who was murdered in the laboratory of the college.

When he was questioned, the suspect confessed to the murder, and later he was convicted of the crime.

It took almost thirty-six hours after the case was presented to high intelligence.

The police investigators thought it had been a coincidence, and we agreed.

For us, a "coincidence" is an act of God, and we believe that we present the cases in this manner to a department of God. To this day, the police believe that we had no impact on the case, that what happened was going to happen anyway, with us or without us.

Our experience indicates that high intelligence chose to solve this case.

Note: You can learn more about this murder case in a new book authored by Alan Burton and Chuck Lanehart, published by Texas Tech University Press.

The book, *Fatal Exam: Solving Lubbock's Greatest Murder Mystery*, includes this story of José Silva's help in solving the case.

You can buy a copy of the book from Texas Tech University Press as well as Amazon and other booksellers.

PART THREE

EXPLANATIONS

CHAPTER 14

We Are Fingers on the Hand of God

José Silva said something puzzled him:

"If God is all powerful, then why did He create us?"

After analyzing his research and his life experiences, he concluded that God created us so that we could represent Him here and do the work that needs to be done in the physical world.

God is spiritual, not physical. Detecting physical problems and doing physical work requires a physical body.

So we were created to be the eyes and ears for higher intelligence, to detect problems and send information back to "headquarters."

We offer our recommendations on the best way to correct the problems, and higher intelligence can confirm, or can offer a better solution.

Then we take action.

If you want to be close to the Creator, that is how to do it.

"A person who solves any kind of problem is helping the Creator with creation," José Silva said, "so the more problems we learn to solve, the closer we will be to the Creator, on the Creator's side.

"The more problems we cause," he continued, "the further away we get from the Creator.

"We can be closer to the Creator by solving problems than we can by praying all day.

"When we get to a point where we will be able to solve all problems on this planet, we will then be gods of this planet, the way God is of the universe."

A problem is anything that hurts the Creator's creation, including his creatures.

Use the MentalVideo to let your tutor know of a problem that we have here on earth, and how you think it should be corrected. Then higher intelligence will let us know, through "coincidences," how to proceed.

They will send us help and will encourage us when we are doing what they want done, and they may put up roadblocks to redirect us when they want us to do it another way.

Why We Do This at Night

When you go to sleep, your brain activity slows down into brain frequency levels that scientists have labeled with letters from the Greek alphabet: First is beta when we are awake and active in the physical world. Then come alpha, theta, and delta, which are associated with light, medium, and deep levels of sleep.

Beta is a full octave, 14 to 21 cycles per second of electrical pulsations. It is made up of seven frequencies the same way a musical scale is made up of seven notes. You repeat the first note to give you the full octave of eight.

Alpha is a full octave, 7 to 14 cycles per second. Theta tops out at 7 cycles per second, so it appears to be the first octave of brain frequencies.

But delta is different. It is only half an octave, and that half an octave seems to overlap theta.

Mr. Silva said that the rest of delta is on the "other side." It's off the chart. It's not in the objective, physical, dimension, where we function in beta.

It is not in the subjective, mental, dimension, where we can learn to function in alpha and theta.

It is off the chart. It is outside the physical/mental world. It is a totally non-physical thing. It is a place where higher intelligence resides, not us.

We function and have dominion in the objective and the subjective. Higher intelligence is on the other side.

Here is a chart he developed to illustrate this.

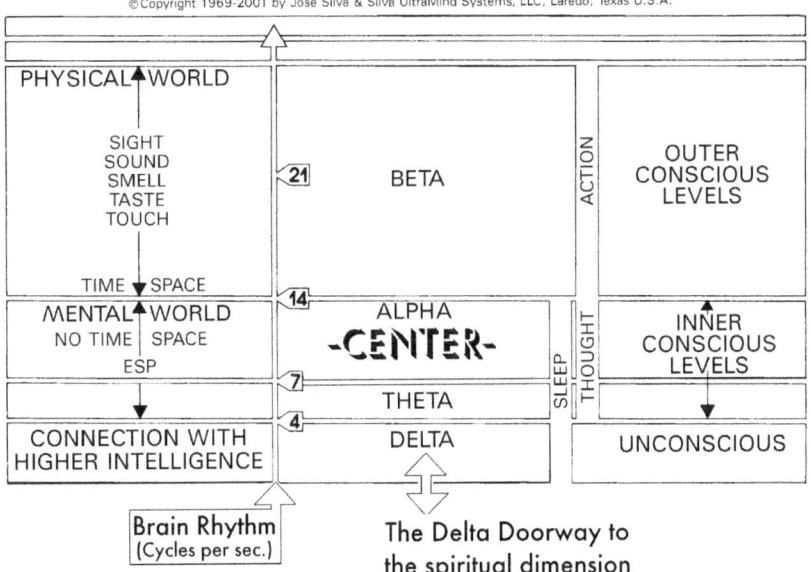

Mr. Silva says that we begin life by entering through the delta doorway. The first human brainwave-type frequencies detected from a child in the womb are delta. This happens a few weeks after conception.

He says that is when the soul or consciousness enters the fetus. He calls it the delta doorway.

He says that once the soul enters the body, through the delta doorway, it centers itself in alpha, where it can function throughout the entire range of brain frequencies. Then it can operate the body much like a hand puppet. Higher intelligence will guide and direct us into what to do.

When a person dies, brain frequency slows, and we exit through the delta doorway. The last frequencies detected when a human being dies are the delta frequencies.

That seems to be how we move from the other side to this dimension, the objective world, and then go back where we came from at the end of our mission.

We're sent here for a mission. How do we know what that mission is?

Our Mission on Earth

Again, Mr. Silva's research and experiences indicate to him that that mission is to correct problems on the planet. That is our job.

Higher intelligence created the planet, created everything that's here, and it is still evolving. We are still learning. We are still developing new things to improve the quality of life. We are still searching for ways to stop destroying one another.

This, Mr. Silva says, is what our mission is:

To solve problems and help convert the planet into a paradise.

People who do this are the people who are the most success-ful. They are not always the richest. That's not always the way to measure success, but let's do what we were sent here to do.

To help us with that, he included in the course what he refers to as the Laws of Programming. They are covered in Chapter 3.

A law, according to the dictionary, is something that is laid down. It is not optional, not something you can take or leave. If you want a successful life, if you want higher intelligence to help you and guide you, you need to obey these laws.

You can have the full power of higher intelligence working for you, helping you to achieve the things you set out to achieve, pro-vided that the things you want to achieve are the same things that higher intelligence wants done.

If you're doing what higher intelligence wants done on the planet, then you will get help from higher intelligence.

Whatever higher intelligence has planned, we carry out.

CHAPTER 15

Are There Limitations to the MentalVideo?

"We don't batter down doors. If you keep encountering obstacles, then back up and look around, you might see another door that will open easily for you."

—JOSÉ SILVA

Two Biggest Problems

The two biggest problems I've seen are:

- Not recognizing the "indication" when it comes
- Interpreting the indication

Recognizing the Indications: When we first started teaching the MentalVideo Technique, I noticed that many people were not recognizing the indications.

They would tell me about things happening in their life, and I would notice something and ask if it might relate to the problem they were seeking help with, and that was often the case.

It was a little different for me. I would say, "I just came up with a great idea that will solve the problem."

Eventually I learned to ask myself, "What makes you think it is *your* idea?"

Now I say, "An idea came to me . . ."

Interpreting Indications can be challenging sometimes, like the time when José Silva had a dream that highlighted several numbers. He thought it was an indication that somebody had an important message for him. So he began searching for that person.

He looked up phone numbers and street addresses, and he even drove around for several hours looking for a license plate with those numbers, planning to stop the car and ask the driver, "Do you have a message for me?"

All of those efforts proved futile, and he came up empty.

He was probably the only man on the Texas-Mexico border who wouldn't have immediately thought of the Mexican Lottery.

A friend who came by to see him late in the day suggested the lottery, and they immediately headed to Nuevo Laredo, Mexico, and found a ticket with that number.

It paid him the equivalent of two years' salary.

Help Each Other Learn

One of the best ways to learn new life skills is through observation. That's why this book includes examples and case studies showing you what other people have done.

You can team up with one or more friends to help you continue learning. Tell them about your successes, and give them a copy of this book so they can learn to influence the coincidences in their life.

Then they can help you recognize and understand indications you receive.

You can do the same for them. Sometimes we learn more from observing what other people do—right or wrong—than from our own experiences.

How to Avoid Problems

Remember that you are using the MentalVideo to communicate with God, and we don't want to abuse the privilege.

Mr. Silva said, "It is not our place to put God to work. We were sent here to correct problems. If we have tried to correct a problem and are unable to, then we qualify to ask for help."

It seems to us that it is better to avoid problems in the first place. We can do that by making good decisions.

José Silva is no longer here so we can't ask him directly, but we found a video of him saying the same thing: "Intelligence prevents problems."

So we also use the MentalVideo to make sure we are making the best decision.

Sometimes it is obvious what needs to be done, so we just do it.

Other times we have more than one good option. In those cases, I am likely to use the MentalVideo—not to ask for help, but to send a report about the problem and what I plan to do to solve it.

My attitude is, "This is what I am going to do unless you show me a better way that you want me to pursue."

Some Things to Consider

Also remember the Laws of Programming. The MentalVideo is not intended to help us get what we want. Its purpose is to help us do what God sent us here to do, and that is to correct problems, relieve suffering, and improve living conditions on the planet.

Good intentions aren't enough. Actions are what count. There are plenty of people who promise to give half their winnings to charity if we will just tell them how to use ESP to pick the winning lottery number. I tell them: "If I knew how, why would I tell you?" I advise them to "only ask people who have done it repeatedly."

Sometimes higher intelligence might not want you to do whatever it is you are working on. One of the most difficult things about the MentalVideo, I think, is accepting the guidance when it is not what we want to hear.

Sometimes people ask about how many projects they can work on at one time.

It is usually best to start with just the most important project that you need help with—the one that is most urgent, or will benefit the most people. When you are satisfied that you have had some success with the MentalVideo Technique, then try including more than one project.

Objective Indications of How to Proceed

Always let your results guide you.

Remember that the indications come in the physical world, something you—and anybody else—can see with your physical eyes. You also need to understand what it indicates.

When you see progress, go to level and analyze what you did and do more of it. If nothing happens after a few attempts, try something else. If things get worse, then go to level and analyze what you did and do the opposite next time.

Some people decide they want to accomplish a certain thing, make a certain amount of money, for instance, or visit another country. It is possible to program mentally to do these things. It is much easier to achieve success when you program to correct problems that are hurting humanity.

If you do not have enough money to pay your bills and take care of yourself and your family, that is a problem. If you have plenty of money and just want more, that is not a problem and higher intelligence is not going to help you.

Higher intelligence sent us here to correct problems, to relieve suffering and improve conditions on the planet. They will give us all of the guidance and help that we need to do that.

The guidance—the "coincidences"—are what Mr. Silva called "indications" that you can see with your eyes, in the physical world. They are visible to anybody who is looking.

For instance, if you want to maintain good health, you might think that a certain kind of exercise would be best for you. However, if you are not making progress, then you can seek guidance.

As an example, I tried for a long time to jog, but never could go very far, probably because of damage done to my central nervous system by the polio virus when I was five years old. Then I discovered that I could ride a bicycle all day, and this produced great benefits for me.

In a situation like that, if you were to create a MentalVideo of yourself jogging but not getting results, then perhaps you would get an "indication" the next day in the form of somebody telling you how much benefit they get from riding a bicycle. Or you might see someone riding a bicycle down the street, and a few minutes later see somebody else with a bicycle. As we say, "Look for indications that point to the solution."

When you think that you have seen an indication, then act on it and notice your results. Always let your results guide you.

Allow Time for Help to Arrive

Here is a case study from a Silva UltraMind graduate in Bulgaria with a valuable lesson:

> A year and a half ago I attended the Silva UltraMind ESP System with instructor Milen Mihaylov. I immediately began to apply it to an issue that had become quite pressing.
>
> My parents wanted to buy an apartment in the town where I lived. I met with a lawyer who was working with a real estate developer. He showed me some nice apartments at a good price, so I called my parents to come to see them. They also liked the apartments so we asked the lawyer to draw up a contract.
>
> He prepared the contract and we immediately sent a bank transfer for half of the purchase price. We were supposed to close no later than three months later.
>
> Three months passed, then six months, and still no deal. Something would come up every time to prevent the deal: the lawyer was absent on a business trip, or the builder was dallying with the documents.
>
> We tried to terminate the contract and get our money back. This did not happen so we filed a fraud complaint with the Prosecutor's Office for fraud. An investigation revealed that a num-

ber of other people had reported a similar experience with the lawyer.

The procedure was really slow, and the outlook to get the money back looked almost impossible.

Around that time, I began to practice what they taught me in the Silva UltraMind ESP System. I decided to be very persistent, and every day I visualized the scene where the lawyer transfers the money to my parents' bank account. I told myself that it was best for all the parties involved, and I knew that was the truth.

I repeated the UltraMind course about three months after I first attended it, to refresh and reaffirm my knowledge. While there I shared with my instructor Milen Mihaylov what I was doing and that I was doing it every day for over a month. I was wondering how long I should continue to achieve the expected result.

Milen told me that I was visualizing the problem every day and was not giving higher intelligence the opportunity to answer. He explained also that in order to synchronize things in the best way for all, it would take time.

He also advised me if in the meantime there was any development on this case I should make visualizations including the new developments.

So I stopped visualizing every day and started observing. Shortly thereafter, the court cases against the lawyer did in fact begin. A year after I had put into practice the lessons learned from the UltraMind ESP System, the lawyer called me and voluntarily asked to transfer half the amount in order to terminate the case and avoid a conviction. He promised that in two months he would return the other half as well.

He did return the first half of the money, but yet again forgot about the rest. Around this time, the last case came to an end and the court issued a sentence for the lawyer—time in jail. At that time his relatives made the necessary arrangements in a hurry, and in two days paid the rest of the money so that the sentence could be reduced.

A year and a half after my participation in the workshop and the use of the lessons learned, the entire amount was transferred to our bank account.

I am grateful to José Silva for creating this wonderful system and to my instructor in Bulgaria, Milen Mihaylov, for his readiness to support me and be there for me.

Learn One Thing at a Time

When you are learning our system, or any other system, it is important to follow the instructions exactly as presented.

It is also important that you don't mix the techniques you are learning with any other system, because if you do then you won't be able to evaluate results.

Once you use our system and start getting some results, then if you try combining it with something else, you will have a baseline so that you can tell if it works better or not.

Keep practicing, use the Silva Centering Exercise regularly to find and maintain your level, and I'll look forward to receiving some nice success stories from you.

Note: You can learn more about the Silva Centering Exercise in the next chapter and in the Appendix.

CHAPTER 16

How to Center Yourself at the Alpha Level

José Silva discovered an area tucked away between Conscious and Unconscious, a twilight zone between wide awake and sound asleep.

It is a special place where we dream, and sometimes daydream.

But most people pop back into full conscious awareness when they start thinking about how they can use the information they find there. When that happens they lose the connection to the information.

Psychologists have dubbed it "the sub-conscious."

Writers and inventors call it "the sleeping giant" because people who find a way to use that level of mind consciously are usually very successful, make good decisions, and seem to attract good luck.

José Silva called it the "Inner Conscious Level."

The Inner Conscious Level

"You have learned to do two things in your life," he explained, "either to stay awake or go to sleep.

"This is all nature has taught you to do: to go to sleep or to stay awake. We want you to learn something else:

"We want you to learn how to stop halfway, at the Inner Conscious Level, where you can detect more information and analyze it more effectively, make better decisions, solve more problems, manifest more solutions, and make the rest of your life the *best* of your life."

Several Ways to Find the Inner Conscious Level

There are several ways to learn. Any one of these will work:

Listen to someone read the Silva Centering Exercise to you, relax, and follow the simple instructions. This is the fastest way. There are instructions in the Appendix.

Have somebody record the script of the Centering Exercise, or record it yourself and let your own voice guide you to the alpha brainwave level. See Appendix A.

Memorize the instructions in the Centering Exercise and do it on your own without anybody guiding you. See Appendix A.

Practice simple countdown exercises when you first wake up. That is the ideal time to practice because you are just coming out of the alpha level. This takes forty days. See instructions in Appendix B.

You can also listen to our recording of the Silva Centering Exercise available for free at the Silva7.com website.

Use the Original Version

There are many free recordings online of people reading the Silva Centering Exercise. Some have been altered based on the reader's personal preferences rather than on José Silva's scientific research.

You can get authentic recordings for free, one read by José Silva and another by Ed Bernd Jr., on our website. Just go to the Silva7.com website and listen for free. No obligation, no signup required. You can also listen to recordings of the genuine Silva Centering Exercise narrated by Ed Bernd Jr. at the YouTube.com website.

CHAPTER 17

How to Improve Visualization

The universal means of communication is visual.

There are thousands of different languages spoken around the globe, which means there are many people we cannot communicate with verbally.

But everybody "gets the picture" when you "show" them what you are talking about.

The MentalVideo directs us to create images of our problem and the solution we think is best.

Here is some of what José Silva has to say about visualization and imagination, which he calls "two faculties of genius."

What is visualizing?

Visualizing is remembering what you have seen or imagined, and impressed on your brain neurons.

You can strengthen these impressions by going over them and describing them in full detail and color.

Whatever you have seen, maybe a scene or an object or a person, describe it to yourself mentally, in full detail and color.

Visualizing is recalling and going over what you have seen with your biological senses.

Seeing, of course, is done with your biological senses.

Visualizing is done with your mind.

Learn to use your mind by practicing visualization. This is the first step into learning to function deductively in the inner conscious level.

Once you become proficient in visualizing, then we need to become proficient in developing our faculty of imagination.

Imagination is creating a mental image of something you have not seen or imagined before.

The Mental Screen

Some people imagine a scene in front of them.

Other people imagine a screen in front of them and project their mental pictures there.

Both ways work fine.

What you want to avoid is trying to project mental images on the back of your eyelids and attempting to see them with your physical eyesight.

That doesn't work, and it causes a big problem: It brings you back to the beta brainwave frequency.

During his research José Silva noticed that some people were trying to "see" mental images. That can cause a problem:

Eyesight is a physical function that we use when we are functioning in the physical world. It is associated with beta brainwave activity.

The best place to do our mental work is at the alpha brainwave level.

Eyesight Is Like an On-Off Switch

Whenever you attempt to focus your eyes to "see" something, your brain goes to beta, ready to take action in the physical world.

Once you have found the alpha brainwave level as you learned in Chapter 16, then when you relax and stop trying to use your physical eyesight your brain can go to alpha.

That might be happening when you daydream, when you are not "looking" at anything, but instead you are recalling something pleasant.

To avoid the problem that some people have when they try to "see" a mental image, Mr. Silva created a technique he called the Mental Screen.

"To locate your mental screen," he said, "begin with your eyes closed, turned slightly upward from the horizontal plane of sight, at an angle of approximately 20 degrees.

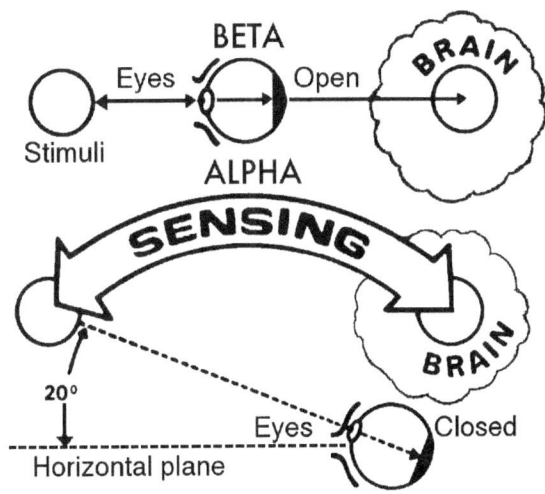

"The area that you perceive with your mind is your mental screen.

"Without using your eyelids as screens, sense your Mental Screen to be out, away from your body.

"To improve the use of your Mental Screen, project images or mental pictures onto the screen, especially images having color. Concentrate on mentally sensing and visualizing true color."

A Visualization Exercise

Have you ever seen a dog? Maybe you own a dog, or you have seen a dog in a movie, like Lassie. Can you tell me what it looked like? How many legs? How big? What color—solid color or spots or stripes or what?

When you do that, when you recall what it looked like, you are visualizing.

That is what you need for success.

I don't have good mental images like some people do, so I just imagine what I would visualize if I actually could visualize. That works.

If you think about what something looks like, you are visualizing.

If you think about what something would look like that you've never seen (or imagined) before, that's imagination.

If you don't have a clear image of a dog, then use your hands to help you visualize it, the way the blind people in Chapter 12 used their hands to find out what my face looked like.

Your body can help your mind do what it needs to do. Raise your hands (keeping your eyes closed) and use them to feel the dog: its size, hair, ears, tail.

You can also learn how to use your mind to help your body do what it needs to do: heal from an illness or injury, learn a new skill, develop more self-confidence, and more.

To do this, you use imagination.

An Imagination Exercise

Now imagine that same dog with six legs instead of four, and imagine where the extra two legs would be, and what that would look like:

- Do you put the extra two legs in the middle to provide extra support?
- Or in the front?
- Maybe in the back. As somebody said, "Now I have a dual-axel Lassie."

That's imagination.

Later, when you recall that six-legged dog, and where the extra two legs are located, and what that looks like, you are visualizing—recalling something you experienced before.

Even if you don't have sharp, clear mental images, it will work, especially when you use your hands to help.

CHAPTER 18

Build Success on a Ladder of Previous Successes

by José Silva

When you have succeeded at something, go to alpha and strengthen the feeling of success. Recall how you felt when you succeeded. Recall the way you succeeded.

Reinforce your success by reviewing whatever you did when you were successful. That's a good foundation to help you keep on succeeding.

We used to say: You reach success with a ladder of failures, to reach your next success.

How we know there is a better way:

We reach greater successes with a ladder of lesser successes.

But always, your foundation should be success.

Not failure.

So reinforce your successes to make them appear more frequently and stronger from there on.

Be sure to reinforce your successes at the alpha brainwave level (which we covered in Chapter 16); recall and reinforce your experiences of having succeeded.

Nobody will know the feeling of success until they succeed.

There is no way to explain to anybody how it feels to succeed. It is a very unusual feeling, when you succeed.

Wisdom is the accumulation of feelings of success. That's wisdom: accumulation of feelings of success. Then, that's wisdom.

Your Strength Is Already Within You

You reach your source by going within, not by anything from without.

We find people sometimes who keep going from one program to another, from course to course, from teacher to teacher, book to book, always looking for "The Answer."

They keep looking, which means they never find the answer. That's because the answers are within.

I do not mean you should not seek help when you need it. But avoid overdoing it.

Techniques are a means to an end, not the end itself.

In the Silva Systems, you learn ways to go within and find the answers you need.

Develop confidence in yourself, for it is *you* who is doing the work, it is *you* who is getting the information, it is *you* who is responsible for your successes.

How do you develop confidence? By experiencing success. Collect as many successes as possible, big or small. Review them at level, and this will help you to develop more confidence.

Techniques are a tool to help you get there, to help you learn.

You will learn that "special feeling" you have when you make correct decisions, and you will not have to use any techniques for those decisions. Only when you do not have that feeling of being right will you need to apply one of the techniques you have learned to help you out.

Developing such self-confidence is difficult for some people. But it is the goal you are seeking. Learn to rely on yourself.

Use your mind and your mental abilities to go directly to your source, for you have all that you need to ensure your success.

CHAPTER 19

Q&A About Applying the MentalVideo

The following are questions that Silva students have asked about applying the MentalVideo to a variety of problems, and the specific guidance we gave them.

If you have similar circumstances in your life, then check the answer for insights that can help you enjoy more success.

If you have more questions please visit the Silva Method UltraMind website, and go to the "Support" section of the website for an answer before contacting us.

Do We Have to Go to Sleep to Use the MentalVideo?

When you are first learning to use the technique, it is best to use it exactly the way Mr. Silva wrote it.

Once you have had some successes and gotten accustomed to it, you have opened those channels, then you can use it any time you need it.

Maybe when we have practiced enough, when our motives are right, when our intentions are good, honest, pure, clean, and positive, maybe that is when higher intelligence is able to send a message through the pathways from delta up to the beta level, where we can become aware of it, act on it, and correct the problem, or prevent problems from taking place to begin with.

Here is an example of how coincidences can take place.

A lady in Australia named Katherine sent us a wonderful example. She said that when doctors saw some spots on her x-ray, they diagnosed them as cancer and wanted to perform surgery right away.

During the night, she had a dream. In this dream, her mother, who had died twenty-five years before, warned her not to go ahead with the surgery.

She needed objective verification whether to do that or not.

She kept looking for indications of how to proceed. She called the physician, made an appointment to come in, and was thinking seriously about canceling the surgery, but still wasn't sure.

She got stuck in a waiting room for two or three hours, just waiting and waiting. She said she got up, went outside just for a change of scenery, and to get a breath of fresh air. She saw a woman, a physician who had delivered her child several years earlier.

She went over and she spoke to her and they began to talk. The physician asked her, "Why are you here?" Kath told her why she was there and that she was concerned and that she was thinking of not proceeding with it just yet because she just wasn't sure of the situation. The physician then told her that she could refer her to another physician to get another opinion on it and see what it was.

The other physician was very busy. It usually took as much as eight months to even get an appointment with him. The woman who had delivered Kath's child for her knew this other doctor. She made an appointment with him for Kath. Kath went there.

"I am so glad I followed my intuition," Kath wrote. "I'm so glad I had these tools developed by José Silva to help me help myself."

She continued, "The new doctor has been an angel for me and my husband. He has spent many hours educating us and involving us in every decision made. He explains everything thoroughly and has helped me deal with all that has come up physically and emotionally. He has helped me and, just as importantly, my whole family through this process. He is a doctor with his heart as well as his profession."

"It turned out I did have cancer," she said. "It is called ductal carcinoma in situ. I did need to have surgery, but it was not as radical as the first doctor had proposed. I have been home from the hospital since Saturday and I'm still medicated quite heavily and not much practical use to anyone yet, but I plan on being better and better every day and ultimately even better than before."

Two years later she emailed us that she was here in the United States and had attended an UltraMind seminar.

Use the MentalVideo program for what you need. Let higher intelligence help you make the decisions. We don't have to do it all by ourselves anymore, folks. We're not in this alone.

How Many Projects Can I Work on at Once?

Q: I have one minor question: I have four separate goals (Personal, Money, Item, and Health), all of which comply with the five laws of programming. Can I include all four of them into one MV session (and later with the 3-Scene Technique) or should I just stick to one goal/problem/situation at a time?

My apologies for wanting to have it all at once. Honestly, I'm on my third year with brainwave entrainment, and I have been trying many other programs as well.

A: We are all different, and there are many variables regarding how fast someone can learn, how much they can do at one time.

Always let your results guide you:

When you see progress, go to level and analyze what you did and do more of it.

If nothing happens after a few attempts, try something else.

If things get worse, then go to level and analyze what you did and do the opposite next time.

I would suggest that you start with the most serious problem, the one you need to deal with first. Make sure it is "within the possibility area," and that you honestly believe it is likely you can succeed.

After you start seeing some progress so that you know it is working for you, then you can add a second project and again observe the results.

When you work on two projects, create two sets of videos, one set for each project. They can be short videos, so you can easily do two or more in a single session.

It is important to have a baseline to work from. Once you see some progress and continue to see more progress, then you can evaluate the changes that you make. If you start programming for two problems and continue to see the same amount of progress, you know you are doing okay. If you see less progress, then you know to just program for one thing at a time for now.

Always let your results guide you.

Remember also that the MentalVideo is not for programming to accomplish things. You can use the 3-Scenes Technique for that.

The MentalVideo is a communications technique, to keep higher intelligence advised of conditions on the planet and what we think we should do to correct them. Then higher intelligence will guide us and help us through "coincidences." The guidance—the "coincidences"—are what Mr. Silva called "indications" that you can see with your eyes, in the physical world. They are visible to anybody who is looking.

For instance, if you want to maintain good health, you might think that a certain kind of exercise would be best for you. However, if you are not making progress, then you can seek guidance.

As an example, I tried for a long time to jog, but never could go very far, probably because of damage done to my central nervous system by the polio virus when I was five years old. Then I discovered that I could ride a bicycle all day, and this produced great benefits for me.

In a situation like that, you could create a short MentalVideo of yourself jogging but not getting results. Just a few seconds should be long enough to show the problem. Then a short solution video of your health goals.

Perhaps you would get an "indication" the next day in the form of somebody telling you how much benefit they get from riding a bicycle. Or you might see someone riding a bicycle down the street, and a few minutes later see somebody else with a bicycle. As we say, "Look for indications that point to the solution."

When you think that you have seen an indication, then act on it and notice your results. Always let your results guide you.

In that example, there is not any need to program to do it. You just go find a bicycle and start riding.

Or perhaps programming might help. If you have trouble finding a bicycle that you can afford, then you could use the 3-Scenes Technique to program to find a bicycle you can afford.

If you still can't find out, then create a MentalVideo to let higher intelligence know about the problem, and look for indications that indicate how to proceed. Maybe you will see a newspaper and find a classified ad with the perfect bike.

Also remember this:

When you are learning our system, or any other system, don't mix it with any other system, because if you do then you won't be able to evaluate results.

Once you use our system and start getting some results, then if you try combining it with something else, you will have a baseline so that you can tell if it works better or not.

Keep practicing, use the Silva Centering Exercise regularly to find and maintain your level, and I'll look forward to receiving some nice success stories from you.

How to Overcome Nervousness and Impatience

Q: I need some help with the 3-Scenes Technique:

a) I am unemployed and it has been a long time. I am looking for a job. How I am supposed to do it?

b) I am also impatient and nervous with my family. I always was impatient and nervous.

Please do forgive my English. At last I took the courage to write and ask for your help!

A: Regarding the 3-Scenes Technique, it is simply a tool that you use to correct problems.

If you are going on a job interview, for instance, you can use the 3-Scenes Technique to program yourself to remain relaxed, to concentrate on what the interviewer is asking you, and to provide the information that they need in order to make the correct decision about offering you a job.

It is not something you use to just imagine yourself having a job and somehow it magically happens. The MentalVideo is a much better tool for that sort of thing.

It should be easy to adapt the MentalVideo to your needs:

What problems do you see that you could correct? What are you good at doing that will help to solve problems and improve conditions and make life better for people? Enter your level and think about that. You will get ideas.

Then formulate a plan, and use the MentalVideo to submit that plan to higher intelligence. Then look (with your physical eyes) for indications—coincidences—that point to the solution.

If you do that, and the next day somebody calls and tells you about a job opportunity that is for something you are good at, and that solves problems and is beneficial to everybody concerned (remember the Laws of Programming), then act on it and see what happens.

Evaluate the results—always let your results guide you. When good things happen, keep going. If you keep encountering roadblocks, look for something else.

You can also use the MentalVideo to seek guidance about being impatient and nervous, and use the 3-Scenes Technique to correct any bad situations.

The procedure is similar for both:

Replay the incident when you were impatient and nervous and you upset a family member, then in the second scene imagine taking a deep breath, recalling your ideal place of relaxation or some other pleasant thing, and responding differently. In the third scene, picture you and the other person relaxed and happy because you are getting along so well.

For the MentalVideo Technique, keep the problem video very brief, just long enough to reveal the problem, then combine what you used in the second and third scenes of the 3-Scenes Technique to show the solution and what you are doing to achieve it.

It is important that you do not dwell on the problem. You want to spend most of your time imagining and visualizing the solution image that you created: relaxed and patient and everybody happy.

Q: I Suspect I May Not Be Doing the MentalVideo Correctly. Here Are Some Questions:

Q: I am still not really clear on what is meant by "converting to a project." Do I actually recreate the video, or is it just a shift in perception to viewing it as a project now?

Then the instructions say that the MentalVideo of the solution contains a step-by-step procedure of how I desire to solve the project. I am not clear on what exactly is supposed to be included in the "solution video."

What do I do if after three days I don't have any indications?

What if I have a problem and I know the outcome that I desire but I don't have a step-by-step solution?

A: Your explanation about converting a problem into a project is perfect. It is just a change in perception. We say it this way in class:

"It is only a problem when you don't know what to do about it. Once you are working on the solution, it is no longer a problem; it is a project."

Make sure your "project" includes all three elements: Identify the problem, visualize the solution you think is best, and include the steps you think will get you to the solution.

Usually it is easier to answer questions and explain things with examples of actual projects you are working on.

For instance, if I want a promotion on my job, I would make a video briefly depicting why I am dissatisfied with my current job, then a few seconds to show what I am doing to improve my skills so I am qualified for the new job, submitting the application or talking with my supervisor about it, getting the word that I've gotten the promotion, and then enjoying the new job.

These can be quick shots of each step, the way you see in television programs. Do whatever you think it takes to get the idea across. And involve your feelings; show what would it will feel like.

If you don't know the steps involved, just depict whatever you can. Imagine you are making an actual physical video to submit to somebody with the power to help you reach that goal.

What would you need to show this person? Imagery is the universal language, so it is the pictures that count, not something you might say.

Also remember the Laws of Programming, and when you get to the end result, depict all of the people who will benefit.

One reason people fail to get results with MentalVideo is that their project does not conform to all of the Laws of Programming.

They might be trying to take a job away from someone else who is also qualified to have that job, which would not be the best thing for everyone concerned.

Mr. Silva also advised us that we do not want to gain at somebody else's loss. So you can take into account what will happen to the person you will replace. Will that person get an even better job? Of course, if that person is not doing a good job, then there are other people who will benefit when you take over and do a better job.

If you don't see any "indications" within three days, there could be any of several reasons. As mentioned above, review the Laws of Programming. Review them while at the alpha level of course.

Also while you are at level, review the things that have happened during the last three days and think about whether any of them could be an indication. If you think that something might have been an indication of how to proceed, but you are not sure, then do another MentalVideo and get confirmation. One of three things might happen:

- something will come along to confirm the first "indication," or
- you will get an indication that the first event was not an indication, or
- you are interpreting it incorrectly.

It takes a little while to get used to it. Once you do, you will catch on very quickly.

If you don't know what the solution or the desired outcome is, you cannot use the 3-Scenes Technique. You can use the MentalVideo, though:

In your video, depict yourself perplexed as to what you should do, and expect to receive an indication from higher intelligence to guide you.

Mr. Silva's idea was that it is not always up to us to make that final decision. We should do what we believe is right, what we think is the best thing, and we should be open to guidance from higher intelligence.

Be patient. It took me a couple of years to really begin to understand and appreciate the MentalVideo. It is not about us doing what we want. It is about us doing what higher intelligence wants us to do.

Not "my" will but "Thy will be done, on earth as it is in heaven." In other words, Mr. Silva pointed out, the plans are already made in heaven; now it is up to us to carry them out here on planet Earth.

Thanks again, and let me know if you have more questions.

Q: Thank You for Explaining Things so Clearly for Me; I Will Try the MentalVideo Technique Again

Q: My project is not an easy one. I am interested in knowing what my real purpose for being here is from higher intelligence. What always does inspire me is getting off work at the end of the day and spending what miniscule time there is left in the day with my family.

For the problem/project MentalVideo, I know I can state the problem pretty clearly and show some pretty vivid footage of myself being uninspired. However, I don't know what my goal is. It is a blank, so I don't know the steps to get there.

A: For the solution video, see if you can picture yourself really inspired and satisfied that you have done something to improve conditions on the planet, something that a lot of people benefited from.

Our "purpose in life" might not be the thing that is the most fun for us to do. In fact, we often see that people wind up working very hard and make many sacrifices in doing things that make a real difference in the world.

That was certainly the case with José Silva. He had an opportunity to be an opera singer. He would have loved to spend more time with his family. Instead, he spent lots of time and half a million dollars (that was a lot of money in the 1960s) conducting his research.

As a result, the church threatened to excommunicate him (he met with them and they backed down), the district attorney investigated him, and friends shunned him. It was not fun.

Even his wife thought he was a witch the first few years, and every time he'd start hypnotizing one of the kids, she would grab the other children and take them somewhere else.

Eventually she saw the value in what he was doing and joined him in his work. She was the one who conditioned the three youngest children.

Appendix A

How to Find Your Center

by Ed Bernd Jr.

José Silva found a simple way to signal to your brain that you are ready to go to sleep, and then stop along the way—before you go to sleep—and maintain conscious awareness:

The Silva Centering Exercise.

Here is how it works:

First you make yourself comfortable, close your eyes, then relax physically and mentally. When you do that your brain frequency begins to slow toward alpha, on the way to sleep.

But before you have a chance to go to sleep, we give you some easy tasks that aren't exciting enough to bring you back to wide-awake beta, but keep you from drifting into sleep.

Here is José Silva to explain how to record the Centering Exercise:

How to Read the Silva Centering Exercise
by José Silva

When reading the Silva Centering Exercise, read in a relaxed, natural voice. Be close enough so that the listener can hear you comfortably. Read loud enough to be heard, and read as though you were reading to a seven-year-old child. Speak each word clearly and distinctly.

Have the listener assume a comfortable position. A sitting position is preferred, but the most important thing is to make sure the listener is comfortable. If uncomfortable, the listener will not relax as much and will not get as much benefit from the exercise.

Avoid distractions, such as loud outside noises. There should be enough light so you can read comfortably, but not extremely bright lights.

If the person shows any signs of nervousness or appears to be uncomfortable, stop reading, tell them to relax and make themselves comfortable. When they are comfortable and ready, then continue.

Take your time when you read; there is no need to rush.

Note: Do not read the headings (in bold print). They are for your information.

Deepening (Physical Relaxation at Level 3)
Find a comfortable position, close your eyes, take a deep breath, and while exhaling, mentally repeat and visualize the number 3 three times. (pause)

To help you learn to relax physically at level 3, I am going to direct your attention to different parts of your body.

Concentrate your sense of awareness on your scalp, the skin that covers your head; you will detect a fine vibration, a tingling sensation, a feeling of warmth caused by circulation. (pause) Now release and completely relax all tensions and ligament pressures from this part of your head and place it in a deep state of relaxation that will grow deeper as we continue. (pause)

Concentrate your sense of awareness on your forehead, the skin that covers your forehead; you will detect a fine vibration, a tingling sensation, a feeling of warmth caused by circulation. (pause) Now release and completely relax all tensions and ligament pressures from this part of your head and place it in a deep state of relaxation that will grow deeper as we continue. (pause)

Concentrate your sense of awareness on your eyelids and the tissue surrounding your eyes; you will detect a fine vibration, a tingling sensation, a feeling of warmth caused by circulation. (pause) Now release and completely relax all tensions and ligament pressures from this part of your head and place it in a deep state of relaxation that will grow deeper as we continue. (pause)

Concentrate your sense of awareness on your face, the skin covering your cheeks; you will detect a fine vibration, a tingling sensation, a feeling of warmth caused by circulation. (pause) Now release and completely relax all tensions and ligament pressures from this part of your head and place it in a deep state of relaxation that will grow deeper as we continue. (pause)

Concentrate on the outer portion of your throat, the skin covering your throat area; you will detect a fine vibration, a tingling sensation, a feeling of warmth caused by circulation. (pause) Now release and completely relax all tensions and ligament pressures from this part of your body and place it in a deep state of relaxation that will grow deeper as we continue. (pause)

Concentrate within the throat area and relax all tensions and ligament pressures from this part of your body and place it in a deep state of relaxation, going deeper and deeper every time. (pause)

Concentrate on your shoulders; feel your clothing in contact with your body. (pause) Feel the skin and the vibration of the skin covering this part of your body. (pause) Relax all tensions and ligament pressures and place your shoulders in a deep state of relaxation, going deeper and deeper every time. (pause)

Concentrate on your chest; feel your clothing in contact with this part of your body. (pause) Feel the skin and the vibration of your skin covering your chest. (pause) Relax all tensions and ligament pressures and place your chest in a deep state of relaxation, going deeper and deeper every time. (pause)

Concentrate within the chest area; relax all organs; relax all glands; relax all tissues, including the cells themselves, and cause them to function in a rhythmic, healthy manner. (pause)

Concentrate on your abdomen; feel the clothing in contact with this part of your body. (pause) Feel the skin and the vibration of your skin covering your abdomen. (pause) Relax all tensions and ligament pressures and place your abdomen in a deep state of relaxation, going deeper and deeper every time. (pause)

Concentrate within the abdominal area; relax all organs; relax all glands; relax all tissues, including the cells themselves, and cause them to function in a rhythmic, healthy manner. (pause)

Concentrate on your thighs; feel your clothing in contact with this part of your body. (pause) Feel the skin and the vibration of your skin covering your thighs. (pause) Relax all tensions and ligament pressures and place your thighs in a deep state of relaxation, going deeper and deeper every time. (pause)

Sense the vibrations at the bones within the thighs; by now these vibrations should be easily detectable. (pause)

Concentrate on your knees; feel the skin and the vibration of your skin covering the knees. (pause) Relax all tensions and ligament pressures and place your knees in a deep state of relaxation, going deeper and deeper every time (pause)

Concentrate on your calves; feel the skin and the vibration of the skin covering your calves. (pause) Relax all tensions and ligament pressures and place these parts of your body in a deep state of relaxation, going deeper and deeper every time. (pause)

To enter a deeper, healthier level of mind, concentrate on your toes. (pause) Enter a deeper, healthier level of mind.

To enter a deeper, healthier level of mind, concentrate on the soles of your feet. (pause) Enter a deeper, healthier level of mind. (pause)

To enter a deeper, healthier level of mind, concentrate on the heels of your feet. (pause) Enter a deeper, healthier level of mind. (pause)

Now cause your feet to feel as though they do not belong to your body. (pause)

Feel your feet as though they do not belong to your body. (pause)

Your feet feel as though they do not belong to your body. (pause)

Your feet, ankles, calves, and knees feel as though they do not belong to your body. (pause)

Your feet, ankles, calves, knees, thighs, waist, shoulders, arms, and hands feel as though they do not belong to your body. (pause)

You are now at a deeper, healthier level of mind, deeper than before.

This is your physical relaxation level 3. Whenever you mentally repeat and visualize the number 3, your body will relax as completely as you are now, and more so every time you practice.

Deepening (Mental Relaxation at Level 2)

To enter the mental relaxation level 2, mentally repeat and visualize the number 2 several times, and you are at level 2, a deeper level than 3. (pause) Level 2 is for mental relaxation, where noises will not distract you. Instead, noises will help you to relax mentally more and more.

To help you learn to relax mentally at level 2, I am going to call your attention to different passive scenes. Visualizing any scene that makes you tranquil and passive will help you relax mentally.

Your being at the beach on a nice summer day may be a tranquil and passive scene for you. (pause)

A day out fishing may be a tranquil and passive scene for you. (pause)

A tranquil and passive scene for you may be a walk through the woods on a beautiful summer day, when the breeze is just right, where there are tall shade trees, beautiful flowers, a very blue sky, an occasional white cloud, birds singing in the distance, even squirrels playing on the tree limbs. Hear birds singing in the distance. (pause)

This is mental relaxation level 2, where noises will not distract you.

To enhance mental relaxation at level 2, practice visualizing tranquil and passive scenes.

To Enter Your Center

To enter level 1, mentally repeat and visualize the number 1 several times. (pause)

You are now at level 1, the basic level where you can function from your center.

Deepening Exercises

To enter deeper, healthier levels of mind, practice with the countdown-deepening exercises.

To deepen, count downward from 25 to 1, or from 50 to 1, or from 100 to 1. When you reach the count of 1, you will have reached a deeper, healthier level of mind, deeper than before.

You will always have full control and complete dominion over your faculties and senses at all levels of the mind, including the outer conscious level.

When to Practice

The best time to practice the countdown-deepening exercises is in the morning when you wake up. Remain in bed at least five minutes practicing the countdown-deepening exercises.

The second best time to practice is at night, when you are ready to retire.

The third best time to practice is at noon after lunch.

Five minutes of practice is good; ten minutes is very good; fifteen minutes is excellent.

To practice once a day is good; two times a day is very good; and three times a day is excellent.

If you have a health problem, practice for fifteen minutes, three times a day.

To Come Out of Levels

To come out of any level of the mind, count to yourself mentally from 1 to 5 and tell yourself that at the count of 5 you will open your eyes and be wide awake, feeling fine and in perfect health, feeling better than before.

Then proceed to count slowly from 1 to 2, then to 3, and at the count of 3 mentally remind yourself that at the count of 5 you will open your eyes, be wide awake, feeling fine and in prefect health, feeling better than before.

Proceed to count slowly to 4, then to 5. At the count of 5 and with your eyes open, mentally tell yourself, "I am wide awake, feeling fine, and in perfect health, feeling better than before. And this is so."

Deepening (Routine Cycle)

To help you enter a deeper, healthier level of mind, I am going to count from 10 to 1. On each descending number, you will feel yourself going deeper and you will enter a deeper, healthier level of mind.

10—9, feel going deeper,

8—7—6, deeper and deeper,

5—4—3, deeper and deeper,

2—1

You are now at a deeper, healthier level of mind, deeper than before.

You may enter a deeper, healthier level of mind by simply relaxing your eyelids. Relax your eyelids. (pause) Feel how relaxed they are. (pause) Allow this feeling of relaxation to flow slowly downward throughout your body, all the way down to your toes. (pause)

It is a wonderful feeling to be deeply relaxed, a very healthy state of being.

To help you enter a deeper, healthier level of mind, I am going to count from 1 to 3. At that moment, you will project yourself mentally to your ideal place of relaxation. I will then stop talking to you, and when you next hear my voice, one hour of time will have elapsed at this level of mind. My voice will not startle you; you will take a deep breath, relax, and go deeper.

1—(pause)—2—(pause)—3. Project yourself mentally to your ideal place of relaxation until you hear my voice again. Relax. (Lecturer: remain silent for about thirty seconds.)

Relax. (pause) Take a deep breath and as you exhale, relax and go deeper. (pause)

Rapport

You will continue to listen to my voice; you will continue to follow the instructions at this level of the mind and any other level, including the outer conscious level. This is for your benefit; you desire it, and it is so.

Whenever you hear me mention the word "Relax," all unnecessary movements and activities of your body, brain, and mind will cease immediately, and you will become completely passive and relaxed physically and mentally.

I may bring you out of this level or a deeper level than this by counting to you from 1 to 5. At the count of 5, your eyes will open; you will be wide awake, feeling fine and in perfect health.

I may bring you out of this level or a deeper level than this by touching your left shoulder three times. When you feel my hand touch your left shoulder for the third time, your eyes will open; you will be wide awake, feeling fine and in perfect health. And this is so.

Genius Statements

The difference between genius mentality and lay mentality is that geniuses use more of their minds and use them in a special manner.

You are now learning to use more of your mind and to use it in a special manner.

Beneficial Statements

The following are beneficial statements that you may occasionally repeat while at these levels of the mind. Repeat mentally after me. (Lecturer: read slowly.)

My increasing mental faculties are for serving humanity better.

Every day, in every way, I am getting better, better, and better.

Positive thoughts bring me benefits and advantages I desire.

I have full control and complete dominion over my sensing faculties at this level of the mind and any other level, including the outer conscious level. And this is so.

I will always maintain a perfectly healthy body and mind.

Effective Sensory Projection Statement for Success

I am now learning to attune my intelligence by developing my sensing faculties and to project them to any problem area so as to be aware of any actions taking place, if this is necessary and beneficial for humanity.

I am now learning to correct any problems I detect.

Negative thoughts and negative suggestions have no influence over me at any level of the mind.

Post Effects: Preview of Next Session

You have practiced entering deep, healthy levels of mind. In your next session, you will enter a deeper, healthier level of mind, faster and easier than this time.

Post Effects: Standard

Every time you function at these levels of the mind, you will receive beneficial effects physically and mentally.

You may use these levels of the mind to help yourself physically and mentally.

You may use these levels of the mind to help your loved ones, physically and mentally.

You may use these levels of the mind to help any human being who needs help, physically and mentally.

You will never use these levels of the mind to harm any human being; if this be your intention, you will not be able to function within these levels of the mind.

You will always use these levels of the mind in a constructive, creative manner for all that is good, honest, pure, clean, and positive. And this is so.

You will continue to strive to take part in constructive and creative activities to make this a better world to live in, so that when we move on, we shall have left behind a better world for those who follow. You will consider the whole of humanity, depending on their ages, as fathers or mothers, brothers or sisters, sons or daughters. You are a superior human being; you have greater understanding, compassion, and patience with others.

Bringout

In a moment, I am going to count from 1 to 5. At that moment, you will open your eyes, be wide awake, feeling fine and in perfect health, feeling better than before. You will have no ill effects whatsoever in your head, no headache; no ill effects whatsoever in your hearing, no buzzing in your ears; no ill effects whatsoever in your vision and eyesight; vision, eyesight, and hearing improve every time you function at these levels of mind.

1–2, coming out slowly now.

3, at the count of 5, you will open your eyes, be wide awake, feeling fine and in perfect health, feeling better than before, feeling the way you feel when you have slept the right amount of revitalizing, refreshing, relaxing, healthy sleep.

4–5, eyes open, wide awake, feeling fine and in perfect health, feeling better than before.

(**Reader**: Be sure to observe whether or not the person is wide awake. If in doubt, touch the person's left shoulder three times and while doing so say: "Wide awake, feeling fine and in perfect health. And this is so.")

It is recommended that everyone practice staying at their center for fifteen minutes a day to normalize all abnormal conditions of the body and mind.

Appendix B

Alternative Ways to Find the Alpha Level

Note: It is not necessary to do this if you are learning by having someone read the Silva Centering Exercise to you, or are using a recording of the Silva Centering Exercise.

I will give you a simple way to relax, and you will do better and better at this as you practice.

I will also give you a Beneficial Statement to help you.

This is how you train your mind. You relax, lower your brain frequency to the alpha level, and practice using imagination and visualization.

Because you cannot read this book and relax simultaneously, it is necessary that you read the instructions first, so that you can put the book down, close your eyes, and follow them.

Here they are:

1. Sit comfortably in a chair and close your eyes. Any position that is comfortable is a good position.

2. Take a deep breath, and as you exhale, relax your body.

3. Count backward slowly from 50 to 1.

4. Daydream about some peaceful place you know.

5. Say to yourself mentally, "Every day, in every way, I am getting better, better, and better."

6. Remind yourself mentally that when you open your eyes at the count of 5, you will feel wide awake, better than before. When you reach the count of 3, repeat this, and when you open your eyes, repeat it ("I am wide awake, feeling better than before").

You already know steps one and two. You do them daily when you get home in the evening. Add a countdown, a peaceful scene, and a beneficial statement to help you become better and better, and you are ready for a final count-out.

Read the instructions once more. Then put the book down and do it.

Learning to Function Consciously at the Alpha Level

As stated previously, you learn to enter the alpha level and function there with just one day of training when you attend the Silva UltraMind ESP Systems live training programs. You can use the audio recordings to learn to enter the alpha level within a few days with either a Silva home-study program or the free lessons at the Silva7.com website.

You can also record the Silva Centering Exercise in Appendix A and listen to it, or have someone read it to you. Or you can listen to recordings of the genuine Silva Centering Exercise narrated by Ed Bernd Jr. at the YouTube.com website.

If you have already learned to enter the alpha level by one of those methods, you can skip the following instructions for practicing countdown-deepening exercises for the next forty days.

If not, then follow these instructions from José Silva:

When you enter sleep, you enter alpha. But you quickly go right through alpha to the deeper levels of theta and delta.

Throughout the night, your brain moves back and forth through alpha, theta, and delta, like the ebb and flow of the tide. These cycles last about ninety minutes.

In the morning, as you exit sleep, you come out through alpha, back into the faster beta frequencies that are associated with the outer conscious levels.

Some authors advise that as you go to sleep at night, you think about your goals. That way, you get a little bit of alpha time for programming. The only trouble is, you have a tendency to fall asleep.

For now, I just want you to practice a simple exercise that will help you learn to enter and stay at the alpha level. Then, in forty days, you will be ready to begin your programming.

In the meantime, I will give you some additional tasks that you can perform at the beta level that will help you prepare yourself so that you will be able to program more effectively at the alpha level when you are ready at the completion of the forty days.

Your First Assignment

If you are using a recording of the Silva Centering Exercise (also known as the Long Relaxation Exercise) to enter the alpha level, then you can skip the information that follows.

If you do not want to use the recording of the Silva Centering Exercise, and you have not attended a Silva seminar or used one of our home-study courses to learn to enter the alpha level, then you will need to follow the instructions here to learn to enter the alpha level on your own.

Here is your alpha exercise:

Practice this exercise in the morning when you first wake up. Since your brain is starting to shift from alpha to beta when you first wake up, you will not have a tendency to fall asleep when you enter alpha.

Here are the steps to take:

1. When you awake tomorrow morning, go to the bathroom if you have to, then go back to bed. Set your alarm clock to ring in fifteen minutes, just in case you do fall asleep again.

2. Close your eyes and turn them slightly upward toward your eyebrows (about 20 degrees). Research shows that this produces more alpha brain-wave activity.

3. Count backward slowly from 100 to 1. Do this silently; that is, do it mentally to yourself. Wait about one second between numbers.

4. When you reach the count of 1, hold a mental picture of yourself as a success. An easy way to do this is to recall the most recent time when you were 100 percent successful. Recall the setting, where you were, and what the scene looked like; recall what you did; and recall what you felt like.

5. Repeat mentally, "Every day in every way I am getting better, better, and better."

6. Then say to yourself, "I am going to count from 1 to 5; when I reach the count of 5, I will open my eyes, feeling fine and in perfect health, feeling better than before."

7. Begin to count. When you reach 3, repeat, "When I reach the count of 5, I will open my eyes, feeling fine and in perfect health, feeling better than before."

8. Continue your count to 4 and 5. At the count of 5, open your eyes and tell yourself mentally, "I am wide awake, feeling

fine and in perfect health, feeling better than before. And this is so."

These Eight Steps Are Really Only Three

Go over each of these eight steps so that you understand the purpose while at the same time becoming more familiar with the sequence.

1. The mind cannot relax deeply if the body is not relaxed. It is better to go to the bathroom and permit your body to enjoy full comfort. Also, when you first awake, you may not be fully awake. Going to the bathroom ensures your being fully awake. But in case you are still not awake enough to stay awake, set your alarm clock to ring in fifteen minutes so you do not risk being late on your daily schedule. Sit in a comfortable position.

2. Research has shown that when a person turns the eyes up about 20 degrees, it triggers more alpha rhythm in the brain and also causes more right-brain activity. Later, when we do our mental picturing, it will be with your eyes turned upward at this angle. Meanwhile, it is a simple way to encourage alpha brainwave activity. You might want to think of the way you look up at the screen in a movie theater, a comfortable upward angle.

3. Counting backward is relaxing. Counting forward is activating. 1–2–3 is like "get ready, get set, go!" 3–2–1 is pacifying. You are going nowhere except deeper within yourself.

4. Imagining yourself the way you want to be—while relaxed—creates the picture. Failures who relax and imagine themselves making mistakes and losing frequently create a mental picture that brings about failure. You will do the opposite. Your mental picture is one of success, and it will create what you desire: success.

5. Words repeated mentally—while relaxed—create the concepts they stand for. Pictures and words program the mind to make it so.

6–8. These last three steps are simply counting to 5 to end your session. Counting upward activates you, but it's still good to give yourself "orders" to become activated at the count of 5. Do this before you begin to count; do it again along the way; and again as you open your eyes.

Once you wake up tomorrow morning and prepare yourself for this exercise, it all works down to three steps:

1. Count backward from 100 to 1.

2. Imagine yourself successful.

3. Count yourself out 1 to 5, reminding yourself that you are wide awake, feeling fine, and in perfect health.

Forty Days That Can Change Your Life for the Better

You know what to do tomorrow morning, but what about after that? Here is your training program:

- Count backward from 100 to 1 for 10 mornings.
- Count backward from 50 to 1 for 10 mornings.
- Count backward from 25 to 1 for 10 mornings.
- Count backward from 10 to 1 for 10 mornings.

After these 40 mornings of countdown relaxation practice, count backward only from 5 to 1 and begin to use your alpha level.

People have a tendency to be impatient, to want to move faster. Please resist this temptation and follow the instructions as written.

You must develop and acquire the ability to function consciously at alpha before the mental techniques will work properly for you. You must master the fundamentals first. We've been researching this field since 1944, longer than anyone else, and the techniques we have developed have helped millions of people worldwide to enjoy greater success and happiness, so please follow these simple instructions.

Appendix C

Additional Resources

You can be notified of our new books by following the authors at SilvaBooks.com or on GoodReads.com or Amazon:

amazon.com/author/josesilva

amazon.com/author/edberndjr

For information about books, products, and courses visit:
SilvaMethodUltraMind.com

Free Introductory Lessons:
Silva7.com

You can also listen to recordings of the genuine Silva Centering Exercise narrated by Ed Bernd Jr. at the YouTube.com website.

Health Cases to work and to submit:
SilvaHealthCases.com

Official José Silva Website:
JoseSilva.net

If you found this book useful and think that others would benefit from it, please consider leaving an honest review at GoodReads.com and with the bookseller you purchased it from. Thank you.